W9-ADR-353

WITHDRAWN

PRESENTED TO
CODY MEMORIAL LIBRARY
BY
KELLOGG FOUNDATION

A Taste of Chaucer

Chaucer, Geoffrey

A Taste of Chaucer

Selections from *The Canterbury Tales*

Chosen and edited by

Anne Malcolmson

Illustrated by Enrico Arno

80102

Harcourt, Brace & World, Inc., New York

Cody Memorial Library
Southwestern University
Georgetown, Texas

© 1964 by Anne Burnett von Storch

All rights reserved. No part of this book may be reproduced in any form or by any mechanical means, including mimeograph and tape recorder, without permission in writing from the publisher.

Library of Congress Catalog Card Number: 64-11493

Printed in the United States of America

B.11.64

C
821.
C392c

For Carol Preston

Contents

A Taste of Chaucer

An Introduction to Geoffrey Chaucer

Thames Street in London ran close and parallel to the river for which it was named. It was a broad and busy thoroughfare in 1350 A.D., lined with the homes of well-to-do businessmen, their guild halls, and even a few mansions of the nobility. A stretch of several blocks was known as the Vintry, settled by prosperous wine merchants. Among these was John Chaucer, a prominent citizen with connections in the royal court. His son Geoffrey, a small boy at the time, was fortunate indeed.

Like most rivers, the Thames provided fishing and swimming, not to mention a steady parade of small boats and barges. In addition, it held wharves and anchorages for the fleets of ocean-going vessels, which brought to England wares from all over the known world. Close to Geoffrey's own home, the Vintry docks received the wine fleets from Spain and Italy, as well as from France. Just below London Bridge, which with its many shops and houses stretched across to Southwark, stood the wool wharves from which English fleeces and woven cloth were carried to the Continent. A youngster with sharp eyes and ears could pick up a considerable education in geography, in languages, above all in human nature, simply by playing along the waterfront. That young Geoffrey profited from these opportunities we know. His delight in observing things and people helped him eventually to become the first great poet of the English language and one of the greatest storytellers of all time.

Much of Chaucer's biography can be reconstructed from official records, but there are many gaps that scholars are unable to fill. For instance, no record of his birth has been found. He must have been born about 1340, but we do not know just when or where. His schooling is another uncertain subject. We know he was a well-educated man with a command of several languages, English, French, Latin, and Italian. The chances are that he was sent to a grammar school where he studied Latin. Many classes were undoubtedly conducted in French, which had been the official language in England since the Norman Conquest. Although it remained the language of the King and of the law, French was beginning to lose its hold. English was now spoken by most Londoners, not the English that we speak today, but Middle English, a blend of Norman French and Anglo-Saxon. Members of a household like the Chaucers' were undoubtedly fluent in both French and English. In later life, Geoffrey was entrusted with several missions to Italy, where he might have picked up his Italian. It seems more likely that he was sent because he had already mastered it to some extent. Just where he acquired this tongue we do not know.

The first historical reference to him is the listing of his name in the state records of 1357 as that of a page to Elizabeth, Countess of Ulster and daughter-in-law of King Edward III. In this position he received an education in the polite arts and graces. He lived at court and accompanied his patroness on journeys to hunting lodges and castles throughout the land. Two years later, during an English invasion of northern France, a Geoffrey Chaucer was captured by the French. King Edward himself put up some of the money to ransom him. By 1367, Chaucer was mentioned as a squire of the royal household. His duties were probably different from those of a squire under the old chivalric system, as these are described in "The Prologue." We know that by now Geoffrey was in his middle or late twenties. We know, too, that Edward used his "squires" and "valets" for government business in professional and even diplomatic capacities. We might today call Chaucer's assignment that of a junior foreign service officer. At any rate, in 1368 he was sent abroad on a mission for the King.

Some time before this journey he had married Philippa Roët, a lady of the court, listed in one official record as Philippa of the Pantry. We don't know very much about her. She was a lady-in-waiting to the Queen, for whom she acted as an overseer of the royal pantrymaids. After the Queen's death, Philippa Chaucer became a lady-in-waiting to Constance, Duchess of Lancaster, whose husband, John of Gaunt, was a younger son of the King and one of the most powerful men in England. Still later, Philippa's sister Katherine, the widow of Sir Hugh Swynford, became the third wife of John of Gaunt. This made Chaucer a brother-in-law of a member of the royal family. He was well acquainted with ladies and gentlemen of the highest social rank, as well as with the middle class from which his own family derived.

From his twenties on, Geoffrey Chaucer was a very busy man. When or how he found time to write it is difficult to see, but he found it. Before his first trip abroad on government business, he translated into English a popular French poem, "The Romance of the Rose." He was well read in the works of the French poets and, by his own account, had already written many short pieces in French or in the French tradition, although these early works of his have been lost. In 1369, after the death of Blanche of Lancaster, the first wife of John of Gaunt and one of the loveliest ladies in England, Chaucer wrote a long poem about her, known now as "The Book of the Duchess." There is some reason to think that he may have been secretly in love with her. It was the fashion of his time for a young man to conceive a hopeless passion for a great lady.

During the 1370's he kept his title as "esquire of the King's household" and frequently was sent to the Continent to attend to the King's affairs. He made at least two trips to Italy, where he visited the lively cities of Genoa, Milan, and Florence and became acquainted with the writings of Dante, Petrarch, and Boccaccio, Renaissance masters of the art of storytelling. Then began one of the most prosperous decades of his life. In 1376 he was made Comptroller of the Customs for the wool trade, an important post in the English economy. It was his responsibility to superintend the collection of duties from all ships carrying wool out of England. One requirement of his position was that he write his accounts in his own hand. He was allowed to assign his duties to a deputy on occasion, for the Court continued to send him abroad on diplomatic errands. Furthermore, he was granted leaves of absence during 1385, when he served as a Justice of the Peace for the county of Kent, and in 1386, when he served as Knight of Shire, or member of Parliament, for Kent. He held the comptrollership until late in 1386 and at the same time enjoyed rent free the use of a very pleasant dwelling over Aldgate, the property of the City of London.

This house had many interesting associations. London was a walled town. At intervals her ramparts were pierced by gates through which traffic poured in and out during the day and which were closed at night. In less civilized days, when raids by bandits or invaders were frequent, these gates had been topped with fortresses, but as peace prevailed, the fortresses fell into disuse and ultimately were adapted into dwellings, not unlike our duplex apartments. Chaucer was granted the use of the house over Aldgate in the eastern wall of the city. From his west windows he could look across the busy town, from the east to the fields and hills of the countryside. Here in very comfortable surroundings he wrote several of his long poems, "The House of Fame," "The Parliament of Birds," and "Troilus and Criseyde."

Chaucer's close connections in the Court had advantages, but they had their disadvantages, too. In 1377 eleven-year-old Richard II inherited the kingship from his grandfather Edward III. During Richard's boyhood John of Gaunt acted as regent for his nephew. By 1386, however, the young King felt able to act for himself. Gaunt left England to look after his personal interests. His second wife, Constance, had become titular Queen of Castile after the death of her father. With his private army, John set out for Spain to enforce his wife's, and his own, claims to the throne of the Castilian kingdom. Meanwhile, willful, extravagant Richard antagonized the Parliament and the barons, led by another of his uncles, the Duke of Gloucester. In Gaunt's absence, Gloucester forced Richard to accept what amounted to another regency. Fortune now frowned upon the members of the King's and of Gaunt's parties, among them Chaucer, who lost his appointment as Comptroller of the Customs and with it his pleasant home in Aldgate. To add to his troubles, Philippa died the following year. There are no other official references to Chaucer for the next two years. What he did is not certain. Some scholars think this the period in which he wrote most of *The Canterbury Tales*, his greatest work.

In any event, by 1389 worldly fortune smiled once again. Richard felt himself powerful enough to oust the Duke of Gloucester and to assume authority on his own. John of Gaunt was called back to England. In July Chaucer was given a very responsible post, this time as Clerk of the King's Works. He was now in charge of all the royal real estate throughout England. He supervised the construction of new buildings as well as the maintenance of existing structures, chapels, lists, hunting lodges, manor houses, castles, etc. This kept him traveling from one end of England to another. Unfortunately, on three occasions within a very few days, he was set upon on the highway by robbers. Whether or not these mishaps were responsible we can not tell, but Chaucer lost this post after a year or so. He managed, however, to retain a place as King's Forester in the royal forest of Petherton in Somerset.

During the 1390's Chaucer lived quietly. He had pensions from the Duke of Lancaster and from King Richard, but even so he thought himself rather poor. By 1399 when Henry Bolingbroke, the son of his old friend John of Gaunt, deposed Richard and became king Henry IV, Chaucer felt himself poor enough to write a

"Complaint to His Empty Purse." He sent the finished verse to the new King. The first stanza goes, in modernized English,

> "To you, my purse, and to no other wight
> Complain I, for you are my lady dear!
> I am so sorry now that you are light;
> Forsooth, unless you make me heavy cheer,
> I would as lief be laid upon my bier;
> For which unto your mercy thus I cry:
> Be heavy again, or else I soon must die!"

The verses were effective. King Henry granted another royal pension.

In 1400 Chaucer rented a house on the grounds of Westminster Abbey. The lease was intended to run for fifty-three years, but in October of that year he died. Because he was a tenant of the Abbey, he was buried in the south transept of the building. This spot has since become known as the Poet's Corner. Many other famous English poets have been buried beside or near him there in later years.

Geoffrey Chaucer was an interesting and very modern man, as well as a great poet. We can estimate his social and professional accomplishments from the account of his life, but we need not guess at his literary stature. In the first place, he was the first great writer to use English in all his major works intended for an educated audience. Before him polite literature had been composed in French or Latin. His own contemporary, John Gower, wrote only one poem in English; the rest of Gower's writings were in French and Latin.

Chaucer was a connoisseur of good stories and an outstanding storyteller. Many of his tales are not original. He took them from other sources in Latin, French, and Italian and put them into his own tongue. In some cases he quoted large passages, translating his sources directly. Plagiarism was not involved. Poets did not expect direct financial return from their works. To give a worthy tale a wider audience was considered a good deed, not an act of thievery. In presenting old stories, Chaucer did many a good deed in more ways than one. He gave life and spirit to the characters, pointed up the dramatic climaxes, and made each tale something new and delightful to his audience.

Being a man of unusual perception, he was able to bring to his storytelling a wealth of detail that he had observed throughout his own rich life. If one of his sources mentioned a lady in conventional terms, Chaucer imagined her in terms of what she wore, what pets she had, what she ate or didn't eat, what she swore by, etc. As a result, she came to life in his writing.

Not only was he a good observer, but he also relished whatever he observed. People, things, customs, activities, whatever he writes about, he writes about with obvious enjoyment. Take food, for instance. On the road to Canterbury, the Host teases Chaucer about the size of the latter's waistline. We do not really need this reference to know how much Geoffrey loves good food. Wherever he has a good excuse, he brings in a list of dainty dishes. Even in the story of Chanticleer, he cannot resist a few lines about the healthful diet of the old widow who owns the cock. Experience of all kinds gave him pleasure. In his position as Clerk of the King's Works, he superintended the building of the lists for a royal tournament. Some scholars think that "The Knight's

Tale," not included here, was written before he held this particular job. It may be more than coincidence, however, that Chaucer's description of the arena Theseus ordered is given in such loving detail that one can build a model from it.

Above all, he enjoyed people. He loved their virtues, their vices, their strengths and their weaknesses. Even when he made fun of them, he was aware of their good qualities. He had the gift of accepting his fellow man without judging him vindictively, a gift that is all too rare. We can learn much from his kindly view of human nature. His appreciation of humanity is especially evident in his portraits of churchmen in "The Prologue" to *The Canterbury Tales.* Very few of his characters, clergy or laity, escape without some wry criticism, but few indeed escape without endearing traits. In the fourteenth century the issues that were later to come to a head in the Reformation had become important. Many serious persons were appalled by the examples set by the priesthood, by avarice, cynicism, worldliness, lack of true piety, etc. Some like Wyclif condemned the lax clergy with bitterness in their preaching. Chaucer, urbane and humorous, did not condone the faults, but still he did not preach. He simply presented a picture of a typically lax monk or worldly nun and let his audience draw their own conclusions. At the same time he made it apparent that he understood the monk and the nun and had affection for them. In a pleasant way he put across his point without recommending that offenders be shipped off to eternal damnation.

If this were a scholarly book, mention should be made of Chaucer's excellence in the technique of versification. Such a discussion is out of place here, for you have only a translation to sample. You will not have read his poetry until you read it in the original.

Furthermore, in this version, there have been many cuts, some of a line or two, some of long passages. These have been made deliberately because this is a "taste" and not a complete translation. Meanwhile, there is something to be gained from a "taste" of Chaucer, an introduction to some of his people and his stories. I am saddened by the numbers of my own contemporaries, extremely well read in many fields, who have never become acquainted with Chaucer's writing. Many have held back by what appears to be the formidable task of reading Middle English. Much of what Chaucer has to say, nevertheless, can bring pleasure to persons of any age who are interested in the world around them. Much of what he has to say will bring satisfaction and inspiration to those who read him in his own words.

When Chaucer chose his design for *The Canterbury Tales*, he used a device popular with writers of days past, that of setting a group of short stories into a larger framework. He wished to include in his work a variety of narratives, of different styles and points of view, typical of a variety of storytellers; thus he created a group of pilgrims bent upon brightening the hours of their journey by telling each other tales. He explains to his reader how these pilgrims met, where they stopped to rest, how they chatted and even quarreled on the road, and gives, in their own words, the stories that they told. According to the plan he outlines in "The Prologue," each traveler is expected to tell four tales, two going, two coming home. There are thirty travelers, not counting the Host and the Canon's Yeoman, who join them on the way. If *The Canterbury Tales* had been completed, we should have at least one hundred and twenty-four tales. As it is, only twenty-four survive, some of these unfinished fragments. Because this book is only an introduction, I have left out a number of the descriptions of the original Pilgrims. For the same reason I have included only a few of the surviving stories.

At the beginning of each tale and each section of "The Prologue," I have included a few lines from the original. In making the translation I have tried to keep the wording as close to Chaucer's as I could. As a result, a number of words that have passed out of current speech have been retained. These, and some proper names that may not have much meaning for us, are explained in the Glossary and Notes, arranged alphabetically, at the end of the book.

Other kinds of explanations, which to me are hard to put into alphabetical form, may add enjoyment to your reading. Chaucer was a chatty writer who assumed that his audience was acquainted with all his topical references, and in his own time he was right. Many of these references, however, have long since dropped out of circulation. His readers, for instance, knew as much about arms and armor as we know about jet planes. But how many of us can tell a hauberk from a habergeon? How many of us can recognize the joke involved in his describing the breadth of the Prioress's forehead? Certain background information that may help you to understand some of Geoffrey's little jokes is contained in an explanatory preface set here before each tale or passage. I hope this may add to your pleasure.

The important thing is that this is an introduction. May I present Geoffrey Chaucer?

The Prologue

Whan that Aprille with his shoures soote
The droghte of Marche hath perced to the rote,
And bathed every veyne in swich licour,
Of which vertu engendred is the flour;
Whan Zephirus eek with his swete breeth
Inspired hath in every holt and heeth
The tendre croppes, and the yonge sonne
Hath in the Ram his halfe cours y-ronne,
And smale fowles maken melodye,
That slepen al the night with open ye
(So priketh hem nature in hir corages);
Than longen folk to goon on pilgrimages
(And palmers for to seken straunge strondes)
To ferne halwes, couthe in sondry londes;
And specially, from every shires ende
Of Engelond, to Caunterbury they wende,
The holy blisful martir for to seke,
That hem hath holpen whan that they were seke.

Originally a pilgrimage was a solemn journey to a shrine, undertaken by a religious person, often on foot or under difficult conditions, to give thanks to God for special blessings, to atone for past sins, or to seek healing for disease and release from suffering. By Chaucer's day, in many cases, pilgrimages had lost their pious character. Springtime and the *wanderlust*, as he hints in his opening passage, provided the motivation for many "pilgrims." Other writers of the day deplored the abuse of pilgrimage, as they criticized the laxity of the church. Chaucer produced a lively picture and included himself among the pilgrims.

Canterbury was a favorite shrine for the English. It lay in Kent in the southeastern corner of England, a comfortable distance from London. Here in 1170 A.D., Thomas à Becket, Archbishop of Canterbury, was murdered at the altar by knights of Henry II. Shortly thereafter the cathedral assumed a special significance. Henry did penance for the acts of his erring subordinates. Thomas was made a saint. Before long, word spread that his relics had miraculous powers. Sufferers who reached his shrine were cured of certain diseases.

Some readers wonder why Chaucer chose to have his pilgrims set out from Southwark, a suburb at the southern end of London Bridge, rather than from London itself. There seems to be a very homely explanation for this. Like other gates of London, that at the end of the bridge was locked at sundown. At sunrise the narrow thoroughfare across the Thames became the scene of a magnificent traffic jam; farmers' carts, merchants' drays, nobles' coaches, horsemen and pedestrians—not to mention the customers of the shops that lined the balconies of the bridge—clogged the road. If a traveler wished to get an early start, he was well advised to spend the night outside the town. For this reason, Southwark was crowded with inns. The Tabard, incidentally, is the name of an inn that existed in Chaucer's day. The Host, who is called Harry Bailly in a passage not included in this book, may well have been drawn from life. There are numerous official records of one Henry Bailly, an innkeeper and local official of Southwark, between the 1370's and the 1390's. He served in Parliament, and Chaucer was almost surely acquainted with him.

When gentle April with his showers sweet
The drought of March hath piercéd to the root
And bathéd every vein in liquor rare
From which the flower is engendered there;
When Zephyr also with his pleasant breath
Hath blown new life in every holt and heath
Into the tender crops; and the young sun
Within the Ram his halfway course hath run;
And little birds are making melody
That sleep through all the night with open eye
(So Nature pricketh each within his heart);
Then people long on pilgrimage to start,
And palmers long to visit foreign strands,
To hallowed places known in sundry lands.
And specially from every shire's end
Of England, off to Canterbury they wend,
The holy blissful martyr for to seek,
Who them hath comforted when they were weak.

It happened in that season on a day
In Southwark at the Tabard as I lay,
Ready upon my travels to set out
For Canterbury, with heart and soul devout,
At night was come into that hostelry
Full nine-and-twenty in a company
Of sundry folk, whom chance had made to fall
In fellowship, and pilgrims were they all

That up to Canterbury wished to ride.
The chambers and the stables there were wide,
And we were entertained with all the best.
And shortly, when the sun had gone to rest,
So had I spoken with them every one
That I had joined their company anon
And promised early to arise and go
Upon the way, as I shall tell you now.

But, nonetheless, while I have time and space
Before I farther in this story pace,
I think it only fair in point of reason
That I should tell you of the whole condition
Of each of them, such as it seemed to me,
And who these pilgrims were, of what degree,
Also of the array that they were in;
And at a Knight then will I first begin.

The Knight

A Knyght ther was, and that a worthy man
That fro the tyme that he first bigan
To ryden out, he loved chivalrye,
Trouthe and honour, fredom and curteisye. . . .

It is possible, but not certain, that Chaucer was deal-
ing a subtle reproof to the knights of his own time when
he drew his picture of a "verray parfit gentil knyght."
By the fourteenth century, knighthood had fallen low
from the great days of chivalry, when it had been ex-
emplified by the members of King Arthur's Round
Table. In early feudal times a knight was by definition
a member of the gentry or higher aristocracy, who held

his land in return for military service, which he rendered to his overlord. He was bound by oaths of chivalry to protect the church, his lord, and all those weaker than himself. During the Crusades many a knight fought valiantly for his king and against the enemies of Christianity. The last Crusade, however, took place in 1291. By the late 1300's many so-called knights had been created out of whole cloth. Wealthy merchants were occasionally knighted in return for a fee. As a matter of fact, as early as 1278, when the royal purse was thin, King Edward I of England decreed that any man of property with an income of twenty pounds a year had to become a knight, whether he wished to or not. For a spoof of the merchant-knights of his time, see Chaucer's description of Sir Thopas, included here. Nevertheless, there still remained a number of the old-fashioned knights, members of the aristocracy, whose careers were devoted to military service, especially in the cause of Christendom. For the particular places in which Chaucer's Knight saw battle, see the entry under "Alexandria" in the Glossary.

A Knight there was, and that a worthy man,
Who, from the very time he first began
To venture forth, respected chivalry,
Honor and truth, freedom and courtesy.
Full valiant was he in his liege's war,
And therefore had he ridden, none so far,
In Christendom as well as Heathenness;
And he was honored for his worthiness.

He was at Alexandria at its fall.
Full often was he servéd before all
Of other nations at the feast in Prussia.

He'd traveled in Lithuania and Russia.
In mortal battles he had been fifteen,
And struggled for our faith at Tramissene,
And everywhere he earned a sovereign prize.
And although he was worthy, he was wise
And, in his bearing, gentle as a maid.
Never a word of villainy he said
In all his life unto a living wight.
He was a very perfect, gentle knight.
But I shall tell you now of his array.
His horse was good, but still he was not gay.
He wore a doublet made of heavy wool,
Spotted with rust marks from his coat of mail;
For he was lately come from far away
And made his pilgrimage without delay.

The Squire

With him ther was his sone, a yong Squyer,
A lovyere, and a lusty bacheler,
With lokkes crulle, as they were leyd in presse
Of twenty yeer of age he was, I gesse. . . .

Under the feudal system, a knight's education began
when he was sent to the court of a lord to become a
page. Here, as a young boy, he was trained in riding and
in the elementary arts of warfare, but much of his time
was spent in attending the ladies, in learning the graces
of the courts—dancing, singing, playing musical instruments, even reading and writing. As he grew into his
teens, he became a squire. He continued to master the
gentle and courtly arts. At the same time his military

education was intensified. He acted as a personal attendant to his lord, both in the castle, where, for example, he carved his master's meat, and abroad on the battlefield. When he had mastered the arts of war and proven himself worthy, he received the *accolade*, i.e., he was made a knight. Chaucer himself had been a page and for a number of years had served the King as a squire. By his day, however, the duties of a squire had been modified to some extent. For instance, Chaucer was sent off on diplomatic missions. Unlike the typical chivalric squire, Chaucer was never a bachelor or candidate for knighthood. In the fourteenth century the word did not necessarily signify an unmarried man.

> With him there was his son, a youthful Squire,
> A lover and a lusty bachelor,
> With locks as curled as though they'd been in press.
> Of twenty years of age he was, I guess.
> In stature he was of a proper length
> And wonderfully light and of great strength.
> And he had ridden with the chivachy
> In Flanders, in Artois and Picardy,
> And borne him well, though in such little space,
> In hope of standing in his lady's grace.
> Embroidered was his tunic, like a mead
> Covered with springing flowers white and red.
> Singing he was or fluting all the day.
> He was as fresh as is the month of May.
> Short was his gown, with sleeves both long and
>   wide.
> Well could he sit his horse and fairly ride.
> He could make verses and could well indite,
> And he could joust and dance and draw and write.

31

80102   CODY MEMORIAL LIBRARY
SOUTHWESTERN UNIVERSITY
GEORGETOWN, TEXAS

So deep was he in love, to tell the tale,
He slept no more than doth the nightingale.
Courteous he was, modest in mien, and able,
And carved before his father at the table.

The Yeoman

A Yeman hadde he, and servants namo
At that tyme, for him liste ryde so;
And he was clad in cote and hood of grene. . . .

A yeoman was a free man, frequently a farmer or
forester, in the service of a knight. Many yeomen were
expert in the use of the long bow from Robin Hood's
day on. In 1346 Edward III used yeomen archers to
defeat the French at the battle of Crecy, as Henry V
later used them at Agincourt.

A Yeoman had he with him then, but no
Attendants more; it pleased him to ride so.
And he was clad in coat and hood of green.
A sheaf of peacock arrows, bright and keen,
Under his belt he wore full thriftily
(Well could he dress his tackle yeomanly;
His arrows never drooped with feathers low!)
And in his hand he bore a mighty bow.
He had a cropped head and a brown complexion.
He knew the ways of woodcraft to perfection.
Upon his arm he wore an archer's guard,
And by his side a buckler and a sword.
A Christopher on his breast in silver shone.
A horn he bore; its baldric was of green.
A forester he was, in sooth, I guess.

The Prioress

Ther was also a Nonne, a Prioresse,
That of hir smyling was ful simple and coy;
Hir gretteste ooth was but by seynt Loy;
And she was cleped madame Eglentyne. . . .

A prioress was the nun in charge of a convent. During
the Middle Ages families of substance sometimes placed
their unbetrothed daughters in nunneries when they
were quite young, in order to provide them with a secure
and gracious way of living, even though the girls may
not have felt much religious vocation. Chaucer's Prioress is obviously one of these, a lady born and bred, devout within reason but rather worldly in her tastes.
Modern readers miss some of the gentle teasing with
which Chaucer describes his charming Madame Eglentine because they do not know the customs of her day.
Nuns were specifically ordered not to leave their clois-
ters except in cases of the most urgent necessity. They
were forbidden to go on pilgrimages. Pets were forbidden. An interest in fashion was frowned upon. The
Bishop's orders were that a nun's wimple, or veil, must
be drawn tightly about her head just above the eyes so
that her forehead would not show. This Prioress chooses
to wear hers in a becoming pleated frill. A nun was en-
tirely justified in wearing a pair of beads—a rosary. One
can hardly help wondering, however, about the Bishop's
reaction to Eglentine's choice of coral for the little beads
and of green stones for the gauds, the big beads used in
the saying of Pater Nosters, to say nothing of her brooch
with its sentimental inscription.

There was also a nun, a Prioress,
Who in her smiles was simple, sweet, and coy.
Her greatest oath was only "By Saint Loy!"
And she was known as Madame Eglentine.
Full well she sang the services divine,
Intoning through her nose full bonnily.
And French she spoke both fair and stylishly
After the school of Stratford atte Bow;
The French of Paris, this she didn't know.
She had good table manners, above all.
No morsel from her lips did she let fall,
So that no drop should fall upon her breast,
For courtesy was what she treasured most.
She wiped her upper lip so very clean
That in her cup there was no farthing seen
Of grease when she had drunk her draught. But
  neat
And nice her gesture when she reached for meat.
And certainly she had a dainty manner,
A pleasant and an amiable demeanor.
She was so charitable, so piteous,
That she would weep if she should see a mouse
Caught in a trap, if it were hurt or bled.
And she had little lapdogs that she fed
With roasted flesh and milk and wastel bread.
But sorely would she weep if one were dead,
Or if men beat it so that it should smart.
She was all conscience and a tender heart.
Her wimple elegantly pleated was,
Her nose well formed, her eyes as gray as glass,
Her mouth quite small, and also soft and red.
And certainly she had a fair forehead;
It was a span in breadth above her eyes,

34

For truly she was of a proper size.
In fashion was her cloak, I was aware.
Of little corals on her arm she bare
A pair of beads with larger gauds of green;
And thereon hung a brooch of silver sheen
On which there was first written a crowned "A"
And after, *Amor vincit omnia.*

Still yet another nun with her had she
That was her chapelaine; her priests were three.

The Monk

A Monk ther was, a fair for the maistrye,
An out-rydere, that lovede venerye;
A manly man, to been an abbot able.
Ful many a deyntee hors hadde he in stable. . . .

A monk, in the strict sense of the term, divorced himself from the world around him and entered a religious
order to spend his life in the worship of God. Upon
entering a monastery, he took three vows: the vow of
poverty, that he would give up all worldly goods and the
pleasures that went with them; the vow of obedience,
that he would obey the rules laid down by the founders
of his order; and the vow of celibacy, that he would
not allow the love of a woman to distract him from the
love of God.

One can readily see how well Chaucer's Monk keeps
his vows. He is a member of the Benedictine order,
founded at the Abbey of Monte Cassino in Italy by Saint
Benedict, who lived during the sixth and seventh cen-

turies A.D. Shocked by the worldliness of Rome, Benedict became a hermit and was joined by other pious young men who felt as he did. According to his rule, his monks were to do whatever physical work was required to keep themselves and their fellows alive and to spend the rest of their days in the worship of God and the study and copying of religious writings. "Austin" refers to St. Augustine, who founded the order of Augustinian monks at Hippo in North Africa toward the end of the fourth century. His teachings included the doctrine that through hard physical work men might come to a knowledge of God.

A few minor points may add to your enjoyment of Chaucer's portrait. The wearing of furs by any monk was specifically forbidden. A loveknot was a knot tied from strands of gold or silver, signifying the attachment of two lovers. A fat swan was one of the rarest and most expensive dishes of the day.

A Monk there was, full worthy of his place,
An outrider who doted on the chase,
A manly man, to be an abbot able.
Full many a dainty horse he had in stable.
And when he rode, men might his bridle hear
A-jingling in a whistling wind as clear
And just as loud as doth the chapel bell
There where this lord was keeper of the cell.
The rule of holy Maur or Benedict
(Since it was rather old and rather strict),
He was inclined to let such old things pass
And set unto the newer world his face.
And I agree, his thinking was not bad.
Why should he study? Why should he go mad

In some dark cell, poring upon a book?
Why labor with his hands, or sweat, or work
As Austin bade? How would the world be served?
Let Austin's sweat to Austin be reserved!
He was a fine equestrian, all right.
Greyhounds he had as swift as birds in flight.
In tracking and in hunting of the hare
Was all his joy, and no cost would he spare.
His sleeves were ornamented at the hand
With soft gray fur, the finest in the land.
And for to close his hood beneath his chin
He had, fashioned of gold, a curious pin;
A loveknot in the greater end there was.
His head was bald; it shone like any glass.
He was not pale as a lamented ghost.
A fat swan loved he best of any roast.

The Clerk

A Clerk ther was of Oxenford also,
That un-to logik hadde longe y-go.
As lene was his hors as is a rake,
And he nas nat right fat, I undertake. . . .

A clerk was a member of the clergy or a student preparing for holy orders. In this case, the Clerk is a scholar, obviously at Oxford University, headed eventually for the priesthood but meanwhile indulging himself in the study of philosophy. Here Chaucer indulges *himself* in a medieval pun on the word philosophy. Literally it meant, as it still means, the study of the nature of the universe. In fourteenth century slang it meant the pursuit of alchemy. The latter, a pseudo-science, was based on the search for the "philosopher's stone," a mysterious substance supposed to have the power of changing base metals into gold, of healing all illnesses, and of giving its possessor eternal life. Chaucer makes many references to alchemy, some straight-faced, others with his tongue in his cheek. "The Canon's Yeoman's Tale" is based upon the tricks played by false alchemists upon the gullible.

As for the Clerk's books, a number of writers have assumed that he actually had twenty volumes beside his bed. It seems more reasonable to assume that Chaucer merely meant to emphasize the Clerk's hunger for books. Before the invention of printing, long after Chaucer's day, a book was a very expensive possession, sometimes costing as much as a small house in London. Only the very well-to-do could afford a library.

> A Clerk there was of Oxenford also,
> Who gave himself to logic long ago.
> As skinny was his horse as is a rake,
> And he was not too fat, I undertake.
> But he looked hollow, therefore rather sad.
> The little coat he wore was bare of thread,
> For he would rather have beside his bed
> Twenty volumes bound in black or red
> Of Aristotle and philosophy
> Than velvet robes or fiddle or psaltery.
> Philosopher he was, but even so
> His coffers had but little gold to show.
> And as for money, if his friends would lend it,
> On books and learning he would surely spend it.

In studying he took most care and heed.
Not one word more he said than was his need,
And that was said with form and reverence,
And short and quick, full of significance.
Resonant with virtue was his speech,
And gladly would he learn and gladly teach.

The Sergeant of the Law

A Sergeant of the Lawe, war and wys,
That often hadde been at the parvys,
Ther was also, ful riche of excellence.
Discreet he was, and of greet reverence . . .

A sergeant-at-law was one of the Crown's most respected legal officers. There were very few of them at
any given time, chosen from respectable barristers with
at least sixteen years' practice or more. They served as
judges of the King's courts and presided over the Sessions, or meetings, of the Justices of the Peace in the
counties.

Before reaching the position of sergeant, a lawyer
often served as a justice in the assizes, i.e., as a repre-
sentative of the King in the county courts. He must
undoubtedly have made many appearances at the Parvise, the porch of St. Paul's Cathedral in London, where
cases of civil law were discussed informally and frequently settled. A knowledge of the sentences, as well
as of the statutes, since the days of William the Conqueror indicated a mastery of both aspects of the English law, the common and the statutory. The common,

or unwritten, law was made up, then as now, from the decisions of the courts—the statutory, or written, law from royal decrees, acts of Parliament, etc.

A Sergeant of the Law, wary and wise,
Who oftentimes had served at the Parvise,
There was also, a man of excellence.
Discreet he was, worthy of reverence—
Or so he seemed, his judgments were so wise!
He had been justice often at assize.
All was fee simple to him, in effect.
His practices were sharp but still correct.
There was so busy a man as he nowhere,
Yet, than he was, he seemed much busier.
He knew the sentences in every case
Which since King William's time had taken place,
And every statute had he well by rote.
He traveled in a many-colored coat
Girt with a sash of silk with markings small.
Of his array no longer will I tell.

The Franklin

A Frankeleyn was in his companye;
Whyt was his berd, as is the dayesye.
Of his complexioun he was sangwyn.
Wel loved he by the morwe a sop in wyn. . . .

A franklin was a free man, a landholder. There has been some question as to the exact position held by franklins in the social scale. Some authorities place them

among the minor nobility below the rank of baron.
Others say that they were of free, but not noble, birth.
In any event, this Franklin is obviously a man of great
wealth and influence. He is the companion of an important officer of the realm, the Sergeant-at-Law. He himself has held various appointments from the Crown and
has served as a member of Parliament.

There was a Franklin in his company.
White was his beard as is the daisy. He
Was fair of face and of complexion fine.
He loved each morn to have a sop in wine.
His custom was to live in luxury,
For Epicurus's own son was he.
'Twas his opinion that in pleasure lay
The perfect, ultimate felicity.
A householder, and that a great, was he.
He was Saint Julian in his own country.
His cupboard never was without a pie
Of fish or flesh, and such a good supply
His house contained, it snowed of meat and drink
And all the dainties that a man can think.
Many a partridge fat he had in mew,
And many a bream and many a pike in stew.
Woe to his cook, unless his sauces were
Piquant and sharp, and ready all his gear!
At sessions he held sway as lord and sire.
Full oft he had been chosen Knight-of-Shire.
A dagger and a wallet all of silk
Hung at his girdle, white as morning milk.
A sheriff he had been, an auditor.
There was nowhere a vassal worthier.

The Five Guildsmen

An Haberdassher and a Carpenter,
A Webbe, a Dyere, and a Tapicer
Were with us eek, clothed in o liveree
Of a solempne and greet fraternitee. . . .

We usually think of trade or craft associations when we think of medieval guilds. There were other guilds, however, formed for religious or social purposes. Although each of these burghers undoubtedly belonged to his own trade guild, they were all dressed in the same uniform and must therefore have belonged to the same religious, social, or civic organization. Guildhall was the building owned by the Corporation of the City of London in which meetings of local officials took place. The Lord Mayor and Aldermen sat on the dais, or platform. Common councilmen had their places on the floor. A tapicer, incidentally, is a tapestry maker.

A Haberdasher and a Carpenter,
A Weaver, a Dyer, and a Tapicer
Were with us too, clothed in the livery
Of an important great fraternity.
Well seemed each one so eminent a burgess
That he might sit in Guildhall on a dais.
And each for wisdom and for mother wit
To be an alderman was surely fit.
Enough they had of goods and property;
Even their wives to this must well agree.
If else, these ladies would have been to blame!
For it is pleasant to be called "Madame"
And at the vigils be the first in place
And have one's mantle borne with royal grace.

The Cook

A Cook they hadde with hem for the nones,
To boille the chiknes with the marybones . . .

In the prologue to "The Cook's Tale," we learn that
this man was the owner of a cook shop in London. There
were many such shops at which one could buy prepared
food, either to eat on the premises or to take home. The
proprietors occasionally hired themselves out to cook for
their wealthy patrons.

A Cook they had brought with them for the nonce
To boil their chickens with the marrowbones
And powder-marchant tart and galingale.
Well did he know a draught of London ale.
He well could roast and seethe and broil and fry,
Make a rich pottage, and could make a pie.
But still to me it went against the grain
That he should have an ulcer on his shin.
His *blancmanger*, he made that with the best!

The Wife of Bath

A good Wyf was ther of bisyde Bathe,
But she was some-del deef, and that was scathe.
Of clooth-making she hadde swiche an haunt,
She passed hem of Ypres and of Gaunt. . . .

Wife means simply housewife. This jolly woman is
actually a widow. She comes from a suburb of the old

city of Bath in Somersetshire, possibly St. Michael's, a town noted for its weaving. Her marriages at the church door refer to the old custom of conducting the wedding ceremony in two parts. The wedding vows were exchanged at the church door; the nuptial mass was celebrated at the altar.

Although Dame Alice, as she is called later in a part of the story that is not included here, is a middle-class woman from a very small town, she has seen a great deal of the world. Too often we think of the people of the Middle Ages as provincial or limited in their movements. Not so this lady! She has been to Jerusalem, the chief city of the Holy Land; to Rome, the seat of the Pope; to Boulogne in northern France, which contained a celebrated image of the Virgin; to Saint James, or Santiago de Compostela in Spain, which possessed the bones of Saint James; and to the shrine of the Three Kings at Cologne in Germany.

There was a good wife; from near Bath she came.
She was a little deaf, which was a shame.
In weaving cloth she had so great a bent
She passed the weavers both of Ypres and Ghent.
Her coverchiefs were very fine of ground;
And I dare say those weighed a full ten pound
That on a Sunday were upon her head.
Her stockings were a pretty scarlet red
And tightly tied; her shoes were soft and new.
Bold was her face and fair and red of hue.
She was a worthy woman all her life.
Husbands at church door she had married five.
Thrice had she traveled to Jerusalem;

She had crossed over many a foreign stream.
She'd been in Rome and also at Boulogne,
At Saint James in Galicia and Cologne.
She'd seen a lot in travel by the way.
She was gap-toothed, in fairness I should say.
Upon an ambler easily she sat,
Well-wimpled. On her head she had a hat
As broad as is a buckler or a targe.
A skirt was draped about her buttocks large.
A pair of sharpened spurs were on her feet.
In company she had a ready wit.
The remedies of love she knew perchance,
For of that art she knew the ancient dance.

The Parson

A good man was ther of religioun,
And was a povre Persoun of a toun;
But riche he was of holy thoght and werk.
He was also a lerned man, a clerk . . .

The Parson is a parish priest, a simple man of the lower
free classes, but still a "clerk," an educated man. He is
the only member of the clergy whom Chaucer does not
tease. In this portrait Chaucer says, in effect, "There are
good men in holy orders, despite the abuses that we see
around us." Too many priests of the time accepted the
income from their parishes but spent their days in London enjoying easy living. There they might find places
as chaplains to trade guilds, which often brought good
salaries and little work. Others were hired under the

terms of chantries, endowments for payments to priests
to sing masses for the souls of the departed.

There was also a good religious man,
And he was poor, the Parson of a town,
But rich he was in holy thought and work.
He was also a learnéd man, a clerk,
Who Christ's own gospel faithfully would preach.
His parish folk devoutly would he teach.
Benign he was, and wondrous diligent,
And in adversity full patiént.
Though wide his parish, houses far asunder,
He held not back even in rain or thunder
From seeking those in sickness or distress,
Whether nearby or in the farthest place,
Upon his feet and in his hand a staff.
This fine example to his sheep he gave:
That first he wrought, and afterward he taught!
Out of the Gospel he these words had caught,
And his own figure he had joined thereto:
"If gold should rust, what then shall iron do?"
For if a priest be foul in whom we trust,
No wonder if a simple man should rust.
He did not put his benefice to hire
And leave his sheep encumbered in the mire
And run to London, unto Holy Paul's,
To seek a chantry for rich merchant's souls
Or find an easy living with a guild,
But dwelt at home and tended to his fold.
To draw folk into heaven by holiness
And good example was his business.
The Word of Christ and His Apostles twelve
He taught, but first he followed it himself.

46

The Miller

The Miller was a stout carl, for the nones,
Ful big he was of braun, and eek of bones;
That proved wel, for over-al ther he cam,
At wrastling he wolde have alwey the ram. . . .

A miller's occupation should need little explanation,
even to modern city dwellers. He ran a gristmill to which
farmers brought their grain to be ground into flour. His
payment consisted of a portion of the grain, a percentage
that this Miller multiplies dishonestly. His golden thumb
is a reference to an old proverb, "An honest miller has
a golden thumb." Chaucer may mean that his man is as
honest as any in the trade.

> The Miller was a stout carl, for the nonce,
> And big he was in brawn as well as bones.
> This was well proved, for everywhere he came
> In wrestling matches he would win the ram.
> He was short-shouldered, broad, and thickly set.
> There was no door but he could heave it out
> Or breach it at a running with his head.
> His beard as any sow or fox was red
> And also broad, shaped like a garden spade.
> Upon the right side of his nose he had
> A wart, and thereon stood a tuft of hairs,
> Red as the bristles on a red sow's ears.
> His nostrils, they were hairy, black, and wide.
> He bore a sword and buckler by his side.
> His mouth was big as any furnace door.

He was a jester and a raconteur,
Although his stories were not very nice.
He stole and made the farmers pay him thrice,
And yet he had a golden thumb, I swear.
A white coat and a blue hood, these he wore.
And he could make the bagpipes shriek and moan,
And with his pipes he led us out of town.

The Manciple

A gentil Maunciple was ther of a temple;
Of which achatours mighte take exemple . . .

A manciple was a steward, much like the modern
manager of a club or the housekeeper of a school. He
planned the meals, bought the food, supervised the servants who did the daily work. Chaucer's Manciple looks
after one of the Inns of Court in the Temple District of
London. There were several such inns, each of which
belonged to a legal society and served as a clubhouse in
which the members could live, take their meals, and con-
duct their business. These inns served also as law schools
for the training of young attorneys.

There was a Manciple from an Inn of Temple
From whom all businessmen could take example,
So shrewd was he in buying meat and fish,
Whether he dealt in credit or in cash.
Now, is it not an instance of God's grace
That such a simple man's good sense could pace
The wisdom of a heap of learnéd men?
For he had masters, more than three times ten,

That were in law expert and clever men.
Of these there were a dozen in his inn
Worthy to be stewards of land and rent
Of any lord in England, I assent,
In any circumstance that might befall.
And yet this Manciple outdid them all.

The Summoner

A Somnour was ther with us in that place,
That hadde a fyr-reed cherubinnes face. . . .
With scalled browes blake, and piled berd;
Of his visage children were aferd. . . .

A summoner was a petty officer of the church, or canonical, court. During the Middle Ages certain abuses were tried and punished by the church, others by the state. A summoner's job was to hale into court persons who had offended against church laws, such as adulterers, blasphemers, etc. To us the word "cake" in the last line of the description of the Summoner suggests a fluffy confection, often iced or having a soft filling between layers, such as a birthday cake. Here Chaucer refers to a flat, unleavened biscuit, much like our present-day oatmeal cooky but larger in diameter.

A Summoner was with us in that place
Who had a fiery red, cherubic face.
With scarred black brows and very little beard,
His face was something all the children feared.
There was no ointment that can cleanse or bite
That might succeed in purging all the white

Pimples and boils that sat upon his cheeks.
Well he loved garlic, onions, chives and leeks,
And to drink wine as red and strong as blood.
Then he would shout as if he had gone mad.
And if of wine this Summoner should take
Too much, then naught but Latin would he speak.
No wonder, for he heard it every day!
You know how any magpie, any jay
Can squawk a "Wot!" as well as the Pope can.
But if a person tried to test the man,
Then he had spent all his philosophy,
And *"Questio quid juris?"* he would cry.
But I know well that he was false indeed!
A garland he had set upon his head
As large as if 'twere for an alehouse stake.
A buckler he had made him of a cake.

The Pardoner

With him ther rood a gentil Pardoner
Of Rouncival, his freend and his compeer,
That streight was comen fro the court of Rome. . . .

A pardoner was a clergyman authorized by the Pope
to sell indulgences or forgiveness for sins that had not as
yet been performed. The money collected from this
practice was used manifestly for the church. There were
a few true pardoners but many false ones. They often
carried with them the relics of saints, bits of bones or
clothing, with which they performed "miracles."

With him there rode a gentle Pardoner
From Rouncival, his friend and his compeer,
Who had come back from Rome but recently.
Loudly he sang, "Come hither, Love, to me."
This Pardoner had hair yellow as wax;
But limp it hung, as doth a wisp of flax.
And thin it lay, in tendrils one by one.
But hood, for affectation, he wore none.
A vernicle was sewn upon his cap;
His wallet lay before him in his lap
Stuffed full of pardons brought from Rome all hot.
A voice he had as small as hath a goat.
There ne'er was such another Pardoner.
He had a pillowcase among his gear
The which, he hinted, was Our Lady's veil.
He claimed he had a fragment of the sail
From Peter's boat, when Peter walked upon
The sea, and Christ saved him from sinking down.
He had a cross of tin inlaid with stones,
And in a glass he carried a pig's bones.
And with these relics, any time he found
A needy parson dwelling in the land,
Within a day he got more money than
The parson could in two whole months—or ten.
And so, with feignéd piety and japes,
He made the parson and the folk his apes.

* * *

Now I have told you shortly in a clause
The estate, the array, the number, and the cause
Why was assembled all this company
In Southwark at the gentle hostelry

51

Known as the Tabard, close beside the Bell.
But now the time has come for me to tell
How we amused ourselves that very night
When we were in the hostelry alight.

Our Host made us great welcome every one
And to the supper table set us down.
A seemly man this Host appeared in all,
Worthy to be a marshal in a hall.
Quite large a man he was, with twinkling eyes.
In all of Cheap no fairer burgess is.
Bold of his speech and wise and ably taught,
In qualities of manhood he lacked naught.
He was as well a very merry man;
And after supper jovially he began
To speak of fun and mirth 'mongst other things,
After we'd paid our bills and reckonings.
And he said thus: "Now, lordings, truthfully
You are to me right welcome heartily.
For I must say, if I shall tell no lie,
I've seen this year no merrier company
At once within this inn than there is now.
Fain would I give you pleasure, knew I how!
But of a pastime I am now bethought
To give you sport, and it shall cost you naught.

"You know that mirth or comfort there is none
In riding on the road, dumb as a stone.
And therefore I shall try to entertain,
As I said first, and give you all some fun.
To pass the time in travel, each of you
Along the way shall tell of stories two
To Canterburyward, I mean it so.
And homeward, he shall tell another two

Of happenings that long ago befell.
And he of you that does the best of all,
That is to say, who tells along the way
Tales of most merit and most jollity,
Shall have a supper at the others' cost,
Here in this place, sitting beside this post,
When we are come again from Canterbury.
And, for to make you even the more merry,
I shall myself most gladly with you ride,
All at my own expense, and be your guide.
But anyone who will not join the play
Shall pay all that we spend along the way.
Now if you all vouchsafe that this be so,
Tell me at once, with no more great ado,
And I shall early ready me therefore."

This thing was granted, and our oaths we swore
With full glad heart and begged of him also
That he would surely promise to do so,
And that he would become our governor
And, of our stories, judge and arbiter
And set a supper at a certain price.
Then we should all be ruled by his advice.
And thereupon the wine was fetched again;
We drank; and then to rest went everyone
With no more words nor longer tarrying.

The morrow, when the day began to spring,
Up rose our Host and was our proper cock.
He gathered us together in a flock,
And forth we rode, just more than sauntering,
Until we reached St. Thomas' Watering.
And there our Host pulled up his horse to rest.
He cried out, "Lordings, hearken if ye list!

You know our covenant. I have your word.
If evensong and morningsong accord,
Let's see who first of all shall tell his tale.
As ever I may drink of wine or ale,
Whoever from my judgment shall dissent
Shall pay for all that on the way is spent.
Now draw your lots, ere that we farther win,
And he that draws the shortest shall begin.
Sir Knight," quoth he, "my master and my lord,
Now draw your cut, for that is our accord.
Come near," he said, "my Lady Prioress.
And you, Sir Clerk, let be your solemnness
And read no more. Lay hands to, every man!"

And then to draw lots everyone began.

The Fortunes
of the Great

The Monk's Tale

I wol biwayle in maner of Tragedie
The harm of hem that stode in heigh degree,
And fillen so that ther nas no remedie
To bringe hem out of hir adversitee;
For certein, whan that fortune list to flee,
Ther may no man the cours of hir withholde;
Lat no man truste on blind prosperitee;
Be war by thise ensamples trewe and olde.

Early in the journey to Canterbury, the Monk is called upon to tell a tale, but before he can begin, the Miller, drunk and rowdy, intervenes with a bawdy story of his own. Whether or not the Monk is offended, it is hard to say. In any event, when his turn finally comes, the jolly huntsman of the Prologue produces a series of lugubrious biographies illustrating the thesis that fortune brings low the mighty. He gives seventeen examples in all, some from *The Old Testament*, some from ancient history as retold by medieval authors, and others from the current events of the late 1300's. These are cut to three here. His theme becomes monotonous. As the Host comments, if it were not for the clinking of the bells on the Monk's bridle, he should have fallen asleep.

I shall portray, in form of tragedy,
The fate of them that stood in high degree
And fell so low there was no remedy
To bring them out of their adversity.
For certain 'tis, when Fortune wills to flee,
No living man her course may then withhold.
Let no man trust in blind prosperity.
Be warned by these examples true and old.

Samson

Lo, Samson, he that was annunciate
By angels long ere his nativity
And was to God Almighty consecrate,
Was a great lord as long as he could see.
There never was another such as he,
To speak of all his strength and hardiness.
But to his wives his secrets whispered he,
And thus he slew himself in wretchedness.

Samson, this noble, mighty champion,
Without a weapon save his bare hands two,
He slew and tore apart a lion, when
To wed his wife he was in haste to go.
His faithless wife knew how to please him so
That she his counsel learned, and then, untrue,
His secret did betray unto his foe
And him forsook and took another new.

Three hundred foxes Samson took in ire,
And all their tails together then he bound.
He set the foxes' brushes all afire,
For he had fixed on every tail a brand.
And they burned all that grew upon the land,
The olive trees, the vineyards, and the grass.
A thousand men he slew there, in his hand
No weapon but the cheekbone of an ass.

When these were slain, he thirsted so that he
Was nearly lost, and he began to pray
That God would on his pain have charity
And send him drink, or else he needs must die.
And from this ass's cheekbone that was dry
Out of a tooth sprang suddenly a well
From which he drank his fill, in short to say.
Thus God hath favored him, as *Judges* tell.

This Samson never drank of mead nor wine,
Nor on his head came razor, knife, or shear,
By precept of the messenger divine,
For all his mighty strength was in his hair.
And fully twenty winters, year by year,
He had of Israel the governance.
But soon, alas, he wept a bitter tear,
For women e'er brought Samson to mischance.

Unto his love Delilah he hath told
The secret: in his hair his power lay.
Then falsely to his foes she hath him sold.
As he lay sleeping in her arms one day,
She wrongly clipped and sheared his hair away
And made him weak before his enemies.
And when they found him there in this array,
They bound him fast and then put out his eyes.

The end of this poor wretch was as I say.
His enemies once held a festival
And made him as their fool before them play,
And this was in a temple, a great hall.
But finally a terrible affray
He made for them. He made two pillars fall.
Down crashed the temple roof, and there it lay.
He slew himself, but slew his foemen all.

Nebuchadnezzar

The mighty throne, the gold and precious hoard,
The glorious scepter and the majesty
Of great Nebuchadnezzar, king and lord,
By human tongue described can hardly be.
Two times he won Jerusalem City.
The treasures of the temple off he brought
To Babylon, where was his sovereign see,
Where he had all his glory and delight.

The fairest children of the royal blood
Of Israel, he brought them low, and then
Made them his slaves, in fetters to be led.
Among the conquered, Daniél was one,
The wisest of them each and every one,
For he the great king's dreams interpreted,
Whereas in all Chaldea there was none
Who knew to what result these visions led.

This proud king had a statue made of gold
Of sixty cubits long and seven wide,
Which metal idol both the young and old
Commanded he to worship and to dread;

Else in a furnace fiery and red
They should be burned, all who would not obey.
But to the order never hath agreed
This Daniél nor his companions three.

This king of kings, so haughty and elate,
Thought that our God Who sits in majesty
Ne'er would bereave him of his high estate.
But suddenly he lost his dignity,
And like an animal he seemed to be.
He ate hay like an ox and slept without,
And in the rain with beasts consorted he
Until a certain time had come about.

And like an eagle's feathers grew his hairs.
His nails like a bird's horny talons were
Till God released him after many years
And gave him back his wits. With many a tear
He thanked God then. And evermore in fear
Was he of trespass and of wickedness.
And till the time he lay upon his bier,
He knew that God was full of might and grace.

Croesus

Croesus the rich, of Lydia the king,
This Croesus of whom Cyrus was afraid,
Was yet brought low from all his swaggering,
And to a fire to perish he was led.
Then such a rain down from the heavens was shed
The fire went out, and he made his escape.
But to be thankful still no grace he had
Till Fortune on the gallows made him gape.

When once more he was free, he would not stint
Till he had launched another war again.
He had done well before, when Fortune sent
Such grace that he escaped once through the rain
And that by all his foes he was not slain.
But now a dream upon a night he met
Which made him once again so proud and vain
That upon conquest all his heart he set.

Upon a tree he was, or so he thought,
Where Jupiter bathed both his back and side,
And Phoebus, too, a towel to him hath brought
To dry himself. And therefore leapt his pride.
And to his daughter who stood him beside,
Who, as he knew, in lore of dreams abounded,
He bade her tell him what it signified,
And she to him this dream hath thus expounded.

"The tree," she said, "the gallows here doth mean,
And Jupiter stands for the snow and rain.
Lord Phoebus with his linen towel so clean
Portrays the sun's rays shining down again.
Thou shalt be hanged, O Father. And the rain
Shall wash thy body and the sun shall dry."
Thus hath she warned him sensibly and plain,
His daughter, she whose name was Phania.

And hanged indeed was Croesus, the proud king.
His royal throne for him could naught avail.
Tragedy is no other manner thing.
One need not in one's singing cry or wail
Aught but that Fortune always will assail
With unsuspected stroke the great and proud.
For when men trust her most, then will she fail
And cover her bright visage with a cloud.

Chanticleer
and the Fox

The Nun's Priest's Tale

A povre widwe, somdel stape in age,
Was whylom dwelling in a narwe cotage,
Bisyde a grove, stonding in a dale.
This widwe, of which I telle yow my tale,
Sin thilke day that she was last a wyf,
In pacience ladde a ful simple . lyf . . .

After the Knight and the Host have persuaded the
Monk to give up his series of gloomy biographies, one
of the priests accompanying the Prioress is asked to tell
something more cheerful. He assents and tells this most
famous story. The tale of Chanticleer belongs to a long
tradition of fables told to illustrate a moral but which
are good yarns in themselves. Chaucer adds many
touches that tickle his audience. The long argument
between Chanticleer and Pertelote on the subject of
dreams reflects a major interest of the fourteenth century. Many writers issued learned treatises on the
subject.

Chaucer must have evoked a smile when he had Pertelote cite Cato as an authority. Dionysius Cato, an ancient Latin author, wrote a book of maxims that was used as a textbook in the grammar schools of Chaucer's time.

Pertelote, incidentally, shows herself to be something of an authority on the medicine of the day. Diseases were thought to be caused by four humors: blood, phlegm, choler (yellow bile), and melancholy (black bile). As she points out, choler caused one to suffer from fever. Melancholy brought on fearful depressions. Her medicine is better than Chanticleer's Latin. His impressive quotation, *Mulier est hominis confusio,* means just the opposite of his translation.

A poor old widow, something past her prime,
Dwelt in a cottage once upon a time
Beside a woodland, standing in a dale.
This widow about whom I tell my tale,
After the day that she was last a wife,
In patience led a very simple life,
For meager were her chattels and her rent.
By husbanding such things as God hath sent
To her, she kept herself and daughters two.
Three strapping sows she had—of these, no more—
Three milk cows, and a sheep whose name was Moll.
Sooty and dark her bower and her hall.
No dainty morsel traveled down her throat;
Her diet was as simple as her cot.
She was not ill from greed or gluttony;
Her only physic was sobriety
And exercise, forsooth, and heart's content.
The gout ne'er kept her from the dance; nor bent
With apoplexy was this widow's head.

No wine she drank, neither white nor red.
Her table was set most in white and black:
Milk and brown bread, in which she found no lack,
An egg or two, sometimes a bit of bacon,
For she was something of a dairywoman.

A yard she had, encircled all about
With a stick fence—a dry ditch ran without—
In which she kept a cock called Chanticleer.
For crowing, in the land he had no peer.
His voice was merrier than the melody
Of the church organ on a holy day.
More certain was his crowing in his cell
Than is a clock or any abbey bell.
For when fifteen degrees the sun ascended,
He crowed so that it might not be amended.
His comb was redder than the coral, all
Battlemented like a castle wall.
His bill was black; like jet it used to glow.
Like azure were each leg and every toe.
His nails were whiter than the lily petal,
His coat the hue of burnished golden metal.

This gentle cock had under his command
Seven fair hens to do his least demand,
Who were his sisters and his wives and who
Were wondrous like to him in shade and hue.
Of these, the fairest colored in her throat
Was called the lovely Dem'selle Pertelote.
Courteous she was, discreet and debonaire,
Companionable, and bore herself so fair,
Ever since the day that she was seven nights old,
That truly she did have the heart in hold
Of Chanticleer, locked in her every limb.

He loved her so that all was well with him.
And such a joy it was to hear them sing,
When the bright morning sun began to spring,
In sweet accord "My Love Hath Gone Away."
For in that time, as I have heard men say,
The beasts and birds, as well as men, could sing.

Now it befell that on a morn in spring
As Chanticleer among his ladies all
Sat on his perch, which stood within the hall,
And next him sat his lovely Pertelote,
Chanticleer started groaning in his throat
Like one that in his dreams is vexed sore.
And when Dame Pertelote thus heard him roar,
She was aghast and said, "O heart of mine,
What ails you that in such a way you groan?
You should be sleeping soundly. Fie! For shame!"

He answered her and said thus, "Oh, madame,
I pray you that you take it not awry.
I dreamed that such a mischief suffered I
Just now that still my heart is sore affright.
Now, God," quoth he, "my dreams interpret right
And keep my body from captivity!
When roaming up and down our yard was I
(This was my dream), I thought I saw a beast
Much like a hound who would have made arrest
Upon my body, would have had me dead.
His color was between a gold and red;
His tail was tipped, and so were both his ears,
With black, unlike the rest of all his hairs.
His snout was small, and glowing was his eye.
Still at the sight for fear I almost die.
This caused my groaning, without any doubt."

"Oh, fie!" she cried. "Fie on you, heartless lout!
Alas!" said she. "For by the God above,
Now have ye lost my heart and all my love!
I cannot love a coward, on my life!
How dare you say for shame unto your wife
That anything could make you sore afeard?
Have you no man's heart, though you have a beard?
Alas! And can you be afraid of dreams?
There's naught but vanity, God knows, in dreams.
Dreams are engendered out of indigestion
Or out of drink or some indisposition
When humors are abundant in a wight.
Indeed, this dream which you have had tonight
Doth come from the great superfluity
Of the red choler in your blood, pardee,
Which causeth folk to shudder in their dreams
At arrows and at fires with glowing flames,
At ugly beasts that threaten them to bite,
At war and strife and monsters small and great.
Just so, the melancholy humor may
Cause many a man within his sleep to cry
For fear of sable bears or bulls of black,
Or else of blackened devils who attack.
Of other humors I could tell you too
That work on many a sleeping man their woe.
But I shall pass as lightly as I can.

"Lo, Cato, who was such a learned man,
Said he not thus? 'Take no account of dreams!'
Now, sire," she said, "when we fly from the beams,
For heaven's sake, take you some laxative.
On peril of my soul and as I live,
This is the wisest counsel, this no folly,

That both of choler and of melancholy
You purge yourself. And so that you'll not tarry,
Though in this town is no apothecary,
In our own yard are herbs which I can find
Which have within their nature, in their kind,
The power to purge you, under and above.
Forget this not, my lord, for God's own love!
A day or two digestives you shall have
Of worms, before you take your laxative
Of laurel, centaury, or hellebore,
Or else of fumitory growing here.
Just peck them where they grow and eat them in.
Be of good cheer and merry, husband mine,
And fear no dream. I say to you no more."

"Madame," quoth he, "I thank you for your lore.
But nonetheless, as touching Cato, he
That hath for wisdom such celebrity,
Although he held dreams are not cause for dread,
By heaven, in ancient books you well may read
Of many a man, of more authority
Than ever Cato had, I promise thee,
Who would deny this Cato's sentiments
And well can prove from his experience
That dreams are prophecies and signify
Both tribulation and felicity.
The very proof is shown in many a deed,

"One of the greatest authors that men read
Says thus: Some years ago two fellows went
Upon a pilgrimage with good intent.
They came into a town upon a night
Where there was such a congregation met
Of people, and of lodging such a lack,

They could not find so much as any shack
In which they might together lay their heads.
Therefore, that they might satisfy their needs,
For that one night they parted company;
And each of them sought out a hostelry
And took whatever lodging should befall.
The one of them was bedded in a stall
Out in a yard with oxen of the plow.
The other man was settled well enow.

"It happened so, that long before the day
The latter dreamt, as there in bed he lay,
That his companion did upon him call
And cried, 'Alas! for in an ox's stall
This night I shall be murdered where I lie.
Now help me, dearest brother, ere I die!
In all haste come to me at once,' he said.

"This man out of his sleep woke sore afraid.
But when he was awakened full and wide,
He turned him over and he took no heed.
He thought his dream was but a vanity.
Thus two times in his sleeping dreaméd he.
And when the third time he had dreamed again,
His fellow came and said, 'Now I am slain!
Behold my bloody wounds, both deep and wide.
Arise up early in the morningtide
And at the west gate of the town,' said he,
'A wagon full of dung there shalt thou see
In which is hid my body secretly.
Do thou arrest the carter forcibly.
My gold hath caused my murder, it is plain.'
He told him in detail how he was slain,
With a full piteous visage pale of hue.

And trust me well, this dream he found full true.
For on the morn, as soon as it was day,
Unto his fellow's inn he took his way.
And when he came unto the ox's stall,
After his fellow he began to call.

"The hostelkeeper answered him anon
And said, 'Oh, sire, your friend has long since gone.
As soon as day he went out of the town.'

"This man began to feel suspicion then,
Remembering the dreams that he had had,
And forth he went, no longer he delayed,
Out to the west gate of the town and found
A cart which seemed prepared to dung the land
And answered the description in the way
That in his dreams he heard the dead man say.
The friend with manly heart began to cry
Vengeance and justice on this felony.
'My fellow hath been murdered in the night,
And in this cart he lieth dead, aright!
I cry upon the ministers,' quoth he,
'That keep the law in this community!
Alack! Alas! Here lies my fellow dead!'
What more is there of this that needs be said?
The people cast the cart upon the ground,
And in the middle of the dung they found
The body of the dead man, slain all new.

"O blessed God that art so just and true!
How Thou betrayest wickedness alway!
Murder will out! We see that day by day.
Murder will out! This fact is surely known.
For right away the elders of the town

Have seized the carter, tortured him so sore,
Also the hostelkeeper even more,
That they confessed their wickedness anon,
And by the neckbone they were hanged, each one.

"Here one may see that dreams give cause for dread.
And truly in the same book I have read
Right in the chapter coming after this
(I do not lie, as I have joy and bliss!)
About two men who wished to cross the sea
For some good reason to a far countrý.
But on their voyage the winds had proved contrary,
So that within a city they must tarry
That stood full merry on a harborside.
But finally one day at eventide
The wind began to change as they desired.
Relieved and glad, these travelers retired,
Sure that the morn would see them on their mission.
But to the one man came a premonition.
For that one man, in sleeping as he lay,
Had him a wondrous dream before the day.
He thought a man appeared his bed beside,
Commanding him that he should still abide,
And told him thus, 'If thou tomorrow go,
Thou shalt be drowned and lost. My tale is so!'

"He woke and told his friend the prophecy
And prayed that he would let his voyage be.
For that one day he begged him to abide.
But his companion lying at his side
Began to laugh and scoffed at him full fast.
'No dream,' quoth he, 'can make my heart aghast,
So that I give up any of my schemes.
I do not give a straw for all your dreams!

70

Your visions are but vanities and japes.
Man can dream all the day of owls or apes.
But since I see that you will here abide
And thus waste the advantage of the tide,
Although it grieves me sore, have you good-day!'
And thus he took his leave and went away.
But long ere half his journey he had sailed,
I know not how nor why his fortune failed,
Yet fatefully the vessel's hull was rent;
Both ship and man beneath the water went
In the full sight of others at its side
That had sailed forth with them on the same tide.

"And therefore, lovely Pertelote so dear,
   You well may learn from these examples here
   That one should give one's dreams their proper
      heed.
   For doubtless many a dream is cause for dread.

"Shortly I say to you, as my conclusion,
   That I shall have from this same apparition
   Adversity. And I say furthermore
   That by your laxatives I set no store,
   For they are venomous, I know it well.
   I them defy! I love them not at all!

"Now let us speak of mirth and cease all this.
   Dear Madame Pertelote, as I have bliss,
   In one thing God has sent me of His grace;
   For when I see the beauty of your face—
   You are so scarlet red about your eyes—
   I feel within that all my terror dies,
   For it is certain, *In principio*
   Mulier est hominis confusio.

Madame, the meaning of this Latin is:
A woman is man's joy and all his bliss!
So I defy my vision and my dream."

And with that word he flew down from the beam,
For it was daylight now, with all his brood.
And with a cluck he called them to his side,
For he had found a kernel in the yard.
Royal he was. He was no more afeard.
He did not deign to set his foot to ground.
He chucked and clucked when he a kernel found,
And to him then his wives came running all.
Thus royal, like a prince within his hall,
I leave this Chanticleer within his yard,
And later I shall tell you how he fared.

When that the month in which the world began
That is called March, when God created man,
Was finished, and completed were also,
Since March had started, thirty days and two,
It happened Chanticleer in all his pride,
His seven wives a-walking at his side,
Cast up his eyes to heaven to the bright sun
That in the sign of Taurus now had run
Twenty degrees and one and something more.
He knew by nature and no other lore
That it was prime and crowed with joyful steven.
"The sun," he said, "hath climbed up into heaven
Forty degrees and one and more, iwiss.
Now, Madame Pertelote, my worldly bliss,
Hark to these blessed birds and how they sing!
And see the flowers fresh and how they spring!
My heart is full of revel and content!"
But soon befell a sorry accident;

For e'er the latter end of joy is woe.
God knows that worldly joy is soon to go.

A black-eared fox, full of iniquity,
That lived for three years in the grove nearby,
By sly, premeditated plan had first
During that night between the hedges burst
Into the yard where Chanticleer the fair
Was wont with all his ladies to repair.
And in a bed of grasses still he lay
Till it was past the morning of the day,
Waiting his time on Chanticleer to fall,
As gladly do these brave assassins all
That lie in wait to murder honest men.
O thou false traitor lurking in thy den!
O new Iscariot! New Ganelon!
O false dissembler! O thou Greek Sinon
That broughtest Troy all utterly to sorrow!
O Chanticleer, accurséd be that morrow
When thou into the yard flew from thy beams!
Thou hadst been well admonished in thy dreams
That this same day was perilous to thee.
But that which God ordaineth needs must be!

Fair in the sand to bathe her merrily
Lay Pertelote; her sisters lay nearby
Full in the sun; and Chanticleer so free
Sang merrier than the mermaid in the sea.
It so befell that, as he cast his eye
Among the worts upon a butterfly,
He saw this traitor fox that lay so low.
At this he had no more desire to crow,
But up he jumped, and "Cok! Cok!" then he cried,
As one that in his heart was sore afraid.

It is but nature in a beast to flee
When once he spies him, from his enemy,
Though ne'er before he's seen him with his eye.

When Chanticleer his enemy did spy,
He would have fled, but that the fox anon
Said, "Gentle sire, alas! Why do you run?
Are you afraid of me that am your friend?
Now certainly I should be worse than fiend
If I to you wished harm or villainy.
I have not come your secrets to espy.
But honestly I swear, the only thing
That brings me here is just to hear you sing.
For certainly you have as merry a steven
As any angel that is up in heaven.
My lord your father—God his spirit bless!—
Madame your mother, in her gentleness,
Have visited my house to my great ease.
And truly, sire, fain I would you please.

"But when one speaks of singing, I will say,
As I enjoy the use of ear and eye,
Beside yourself I never heard one sing
As did your father on a morn in spring.
Right from his heart came everything he sang.
To make the timbre of his voice more strong
He would so strain himself that either eye
Was tightly shut, so loudly would he cry,
And stand upon his tiptoes therewithal
And stretch his neck till it was long and small.
Now, sire, can you your father imitate?"
Then Chanticleer his wings began to beat.
He could no treason in the fox espy,
So ravished was he by his flattery.

Alas, ye lords! Full many a flatterer
Is in your courts, and many a perjurer,
That give you more of pleasure, by my faith,
Then he who tells you nothing but the truth.

This Chanticleer stood high upon his toes,
Stretched out his neck, and held his eyes a-close,
And strained to crow out loudly for the nonce.
At this Sir Russell Fox leapt up at once
And by the gullet seized poor Chanticleer,
Whom to the woods upon his back he bore.
As yet no one had seen the fox's jape.
O Destiny, whom no one can escape!
Alas, that Chanticleer flew from the beams!
Alas, his wife had no respect for dreams!

Such shrieks, indeed, such lamentations loud
Were ne'er by ladies made when Troy the proud
Was won, and Pyrrhus with his naked sword
Had seized the old King Priam by the beard
And slain him, as th'*Aeneid* telleth us,
As did these hens within the little close
When they espied what fell to Chanticleer.
But more than all, Dame Pertelote shrieked clear!
The poor old widow and her daughters two
Heard the hens crying out and making woe.
Out of the cottage door at once they ran
And saw the fox, as toward the wood he ran
Bearing away the cock upon his back.
They cried out, "Harrow! Wel-a-way! Alack!
Ha! Ha! The fox!" and after him they ran.

And now with staves came many a neighbor man,
And Coll our dog, and Talbot, and Gerland,

And Malkin with a distaff in her hand.
The cows and calves ran, also ran the hogs,
Excited by the barking of the dogs.
They yelled as do the devils down in hell.
The ducks were quacking, terrified and shrill.
The geese, for fear, flew up above the trees.
Out of the hive buzzed forth the swarm of bees.
So great the noise, ah, *Benedicité*,
Indeed, Jack Straw and all his company
Never made racket half so loud and shrill
When they were hot on some poor Fleming's trail,
As on that day was made about the fox.
The folk brought trumpets made of brass and box
And horn and bone, on which they blew and
  pooped,
And with it all they screamed and shrieked and
  whooped.
It seemed indeed that heaven itself should fall.
Now, honest men, I pray you, hearken all!

Behold how Fortune turneth suddenly
The hope and pride of him, her enemy!
This cock that lay upon the fox's back
In all his fear turned to the fox and spake
And said, "Sire, if I were as wise as ye,
Then would I say—and may God succor me!—
'Turn back again, you proud pursuers all.
A very pestilence upon you fall!
Now that I've beat you to the forest side
Despite your care, the cock shall here abide
Now I shall eat him, sires, right away!' "

The fox replied, "I'll do it, by my fay!"
And as he spoke the word, then suddenly

The cock broke from his mouth all safe and free,
And high into a tree he flew anon.
And when the fox saw that his prey was gone,
"Alas!" quoth he. "Alas! O Chanticleer,
I have to you," he said, "been most unfair,
Since I indeed have made you sore afeard
By seizing you so roughly in your yard.
But, sire, I did it with no ill intent.
Come down, and I shall tell you what I meant.
I'll tell the truth to you, God help me so!"

"Nay, then," said Chanticleer, "I'll curse us two!
But first I'll curse myself, both blood and bones,
If you should fool me oftener than once.
You shall no longer through your flattery
Get me to sing and cover up mine eye.
For he that blinketh when he ought to see—
God grant no grace to such a fool as he!"

"Nay," quoth the fox, "but God bring him to dole
That is so lacking in his self-control
He chatters when he ought to hold his peace."

Lo, thus it is with those who are remiss
And negligent and trust in flattery.
But ye who think this tale a vanity
Told of a fox, or of a cock and hen,
Take to your hearts the moral, my good men.
For Saint Paul says that any written tale
Is for our guidance, is a parable.
Take you the wheat, and let the chaff lie still.

Now, God above, if that it be Thy will,
As prayed my Lord, so make us all good men
And bring us to His heavenly bliss. Amen!

Patient Griselda

The Tale of the Clerk of Oxenford

Ther is, at the west syde of Itaille,
Doun at the rote of Vesulus the colde,
A lusty playne, habundant of vitaille,
Wher many a tour and toun thou mayst biholde,
That founded were in tyme of fadres olde,
And many another delitable sighte,
And Saluces this noble contree highte.

The story told by the Wife of Bath, not included in this book, has as its theme the notion that the woman should have the upper hand in marriage. During the course of her comments, the good lady insults the Clerk of Oxenford. When his chance comes, therefore, he tells a story that may be construed as a gentle rebuke, the story of Griselda, whose patience and submission to her husband are rather more than exemplary.

This tale, which Chaucer "translated" from the works of Petrarch, an Italian poet, was popular at his time, especially among husbands. A book of instructions written by a gentleman of Paris for his fifteen-year-old bride quotes it over and over again.

There is a plain in western Italy,
Lying beneath Mount Viso high and cold,
A lovely plain, fertile and green to see,
Where many a tower and town you may behold
Established in the time of men of old,
And many a prospect pleasant, wide and grand.
Saluzzo is the name of this fair land.

A Marquis ruled the land, of lineage
The very noblest born of Lombardy,
A person fair and strong and young in age
And full of honor and of courtesy,
Discreet enough to rule his seigniory;
Though in some things he earned a little blame.
And Walter was this youthful Marquis' name.

I blame him thus, that he considered not
What in a future time there might betide;
But on his pleasure he spent all his thought,
To ride and hunt and hawk on every side.
Nearly all other business he let slide.
Also, he would not (this was worst of all)
Marry a wife, whatever might befall.

This latter point his people bore so sore
That in a flock to him one day they went.
And one of them that had the greatest lore,
Or else because their lord would best assent
That he should tell him what his people meant,
Or else since he could put such matters well,
He spoke unto the Marquis as I tell.

"O noble Marquis, your humanity
Gives us the courage and the hardiness,
As often as we see necessity,

That we explain to you our heaviness
Of heart. Accept, Lord, in your gentleness,
Our wish that you should be a wedded man.
Your folk would live in full contentment then.

"Free us from our anxiety and dread
And take a wife, for the dear Master's sake.
For if it so befall, which God forbid,
That through your death your lineage should break
And that a strange inheritor should take
Your seigniory, O woe to such as we!
Wherefore we pray you, marry speedily."

Their humble prayers and all their piteous cheer
Stirred in the Marquis' heart great charity.
"You now constrain me, my own people dear,
To what I've never thought to do," said he.
"I have been happy in my liberty,
Which seldom times in marriage may be found.
Where I was free, in chains I must be bound."

Not far off from the hall magnificent
Where the young Marquis readied him to wed,
There stood a thorp, pleasant to see and quaint,
In which the poor folk of the village had
Their little farms and homes and livelihood,
And with their labor took their sustenance
From what earth gave them with benevolence.

Among these poorer folk there dwelt a man
Who was considered poorest of them all
(But when He wills, the Lord above us can
Bestow His grace upon an ox's stall),
Janicula his name to great and small.

He had a daughter lovely to behold.
Griselda was the name that she was called.

Upon Griselda, this poor humble maid,
Full often had the Marquis set his eye
When on his hunting he was wont to ride.
And when it happened that he chanced to spy
Her, not with wanton look nor foolishly,
Deep in his heart he settled that he would
Wed her alone, if wed he ever should.

The day of wedding came, but no one knew
What woman the young Marquis' bride should be.
And at this marvel wondered not a few
Who said, when they were gathered privately,
"Will not our lord yet leave his vanity?
Will he not wed? Alas, alas, the while!
Why will he thus himself and us beguile?"

Meanwhile, the Marquis ordered to be made
Of jewels set in gold and set in azure
Brooches and rings for fair Griselda's meed,
While of her clothing he had had the measure
Made from a maiden like to her in stature,
As well as other gems and finery
That proper to so rich a wedding be.

This royal Marquis, gorgeously arrayed,
With lords and ladies in his company,
All those who to the wedding feast were bade,
And all the young men of his livery,
With many a sound of sundry melody,
Unto the thorp of which you have been told
In bright array his proper course did hold.

Griselda, heaven knows full innocent
That for her sake was readied this display.
To fetch some water from the fountain went
And hurried home as quickly as she may;
For well she had heard said that on that day
The Marquis would be wed, and if she might,
She longed to see a little of the sight.

Almost across her threshold she had gone
When the young Marquis came and her did call.
Quickly she set her water bucket down
Beside the doorway in the ox's stall.
And down upon her knees Griselda fell,
And with demure expression held her still
Until she heard what was the Marquis' will.

"Griselda," said the Marquis, "understand
That it is pleasing to your sire and me
That I should wed you. May it also stand,
I hope, that you as well wish this to be.
But these few questions I must ask," said he,
"Since all this must be done in hasty guise,
Will you assent or speak in other wise?

"I say this. Are you ready with good heart
To do my pleasure, whatsoe'er I say,
As I think best, whether you laugh or smart,
And never to begrudge it night or day?
Also, when I say Yes, ye say not Nay,
Either in word or frown or sorry cheer?
Swear this, and our alliance here I swear!"

Bewildered at his word, aquake for dread,
"Ignoble and unworthy, lord," said she,
"Am I for such an honor as you bid.

But as you wish, right ever shall it be.
And here I swear that never willingly
In deed or thought I shall you disobey,
Though I were loath to die and you should slay."

"This is enough, Griselda mine," said he.
And forth he went with a full sober air
Out at the door, and after him came she.
Then to the people who were waiting there,
"This is my wife," he said, "that standeth here.
Honor her, love her, all of you, I pray,
That love me. Now there is no more to say."

To see that nothing of her former gear
Was brought into the palace, now he bade
That ladies should take hold of her right there;
At which these ladies were not very glad
To touch the rags in which she had been clad.
But nonetheless, this maiden bright of hue
From foot to head they dressed in clothing new.

They combed her hair, which on her shoulders yet
Fell rude and tangled. With their fingers small
They placed upon her head a coronet.
They decked her out in clasps bejewelled all.
Of her array what should I further tell?
The folk scarce knew her for her radiance,
Transformed as she was thus with elegance.

And very soon, to speed the story's pace,
To this same lovely Marchioness, I say,
God hath bestowed such favor of His grace.
It seemed impossible in any way
That she was born and bred in poverty,

In a poor cottage or an ox's stall,
And was not fostered in a noble's hall.

Not long time after Walter and Griseld
Were wedded, she a little daughter bore,
Though she'd have rather had a son for child.
Glad were the Marquis and the folk therefore,
For though a maiden child had come before,
That there should be a son was probable,
Because the Marchioness was youthful still.

It happened, as it often happens, now
While this young daughter in her cradle lay,
The Marquis in his heart was tempted so
To test his wife and her fidelity.
He could not banish from his heart away
This strange desire to assay his wife
And make her tremble for her very life.

But thus the Marquis acted in this case.
He came alone at night to where she lay,
With stern expression and with troubled face.
"Griselda," thus he spoke to her, "that day
I took you out of all your poor array
And brought you up from low to high estate,
I think that you have not forgotten yet.

"You know yourself indeed how you came here
Into this house. It was not long ago.
And though to me you still are very dear,
Unto my noblemen you are not so.
They say, to them it is great shame and woe
For to be subject and to be in thrall
To thee, a peasant born in cottage small.

"Now, ever since our daughter has been born,
  They speak more openly such words as these.
  But I desire, as I have always sworn,
  To live my life with them in rest and peace.
  I may not now ignore them in this case.
  And with my daughter I must do therefore
  Not as I wish, but as my folk implore.

"And yet, God knows, this is full hard for me.
  Without your full agreement, nonetheless,
  I will do nought. So I request," said he,
  "That you give your assent to what I press.
  Show now your patience, your submissiveness,
  That you have promised in your simple cot
  The day our marriage hath been brought about."

When she had heard all this, she made no sign
Either in rueful word or countenance,
For as it seemed she felt no grief nor pain.
She said, "My lord, all at your sufferance
My child and I, with full obedience,
Belong to you. And you may save or spill
Your own possessions. Work, my lord, your will."

Glad was the Marquis at her resignation,
Though he pretended that he was not so.
All dreary were his face and his expression
When from Griselda's chamber he did go.
Soon after this, a furlong off or two,
He secretly disclosed his full intent
Unto his sergeant, whom to her he sent.

"Madame," the sergeant said, "forgive it me
If I do things to which I am compelled.
You are so wise, you know as well as I

86

My lord's demands may not be lightly held.
They well may be complained of or bewailed,
But one must needs his master's will obey,
And so shall I. There is no more to say.

"This child I am commanded now to take."
He spoke no more. Then with no further stint
He seized the babe. Roughly he seemed to make
As if he were to kill her when he went.
Griselda could but suffer and consent.
Just like a lamb she sat all meek and still
And let the cruel sergeant do his will.

But at the last to speak she then began
And meekly to the sergeant there she prayed,
Because he was a worthy gentleman,
That she might kiss her child before it died.
And in her lap the little child she laid
With a sad face and started her to kiss
To lull her off to sleep and then to bless.

And thus she spoke in a pathetic voice.
"Farewell, my child. I shall thee never see.
But since I've marked thy forehead with the Cross,
By that same Father blessèd must thou be
Who for our sake hath died upon the Tree.
To Him, my child, thy soul do I bespeak,
For thou this night shalt perish for my sake."

I trow that to a nurse in such a case
It would go hard this sorry sight to see.
Well might a mother then cry out, "Alas!"
But nonetheless, so steadfast still was she
That she endured all this adversity,

And to the sergeant patiently she said,
"Have here again this little tiny maid.

"Go now," said she, "and do my lord's command.
But one thing I shall beg you of your grace,
That if your lord forbid not, with your hand
Bury this little body in some place
Where neither beast nor bird may it deface."
Then not a word in answer could he say.
He took the child and went upon his way.

This sergeant came unto his lord again,
And of Griselda's words and her despair
He told him point by point, in short and plain,
And gave into his arms his daughter dear.
Into the Marquis' eye there sprang a tear,
But nonetheless his purpose held he still,
As lords will do when they must have their will.

Now to Bologna, to his sister dear,
The Countess of Panicia in those days,
He sent the child and told her the affair
And begged her that it be her business
To rear this child with every gentleness.
But whose child it should be, he bade her hide
From everyone, no matter what betide.

The sergeant went to carry out this thing.
Now to the Marquis your attention give.
He watched to see if sorrow now could bring
To his wife's face a sign that she should grieve,
Or if in any word he could perceive
That she were changed. But he could never find
Her manner aught but serious and kind.

And so in this estate some winters four
Passed ere she grew with child. Then, as God willed,
The Marchioness a son to Walter bore,
A handsome boy and gracious to behold.
And when this to the Marquis had been told,
Not only he but all his folk were glad
About the child. And they gave thanks to God.

Now when this little boy was two years old
And taken from his nurse, one sorry day
Once more the Marquis felt himself impelled
To test Griselda's patience, if he may.
Oh, needless this fair lady to assay!
But married men, ye know, have little measure
When they are moved to try a patient creature.

"Wife," said the Marquis, "how my folk resent
Our marriage, you have often heard before.
Especially now that a son is sent,
The folk are troubled more than e'er they were.
They pierce my heart with sorrow to the core.
For to my ears now sharply comes the noise
Of discontent, which all my heart destroys."

The ugly sergeant, in the selfsame wise
That he caught up her daughter, brutally
Or worse, if men worse manner can devise,
Hath seized her son, who was so fair and free.
But ever so long-suffering was she
That she gave not a sign of heaviness
But kissed her son and started him to bless.

Again she begged the sergeant, if he might,
Her little son to bury in a grave,
His tender limbs, so fragile to the sight,

From vultures and wild animals to save.
But from him not an answer might she have.
As though he were unmoved, he went his way
And gently to Bologna brought the boy.

The Marquis waited for a word or sign
That she some change of spirit might betray.
But never any hint could he divine.
For she was calm in heart and visage aye,
And as she older grew, she seemed to be,
If that were possible, more faithful still
And true to him in love and to his will.

Now when his daughter was of age to marry,
(That is, twelve years), he sent, in secret wise
Informed of his intent, his emissary
To Rome, requesting that the Court devise
However for his purpose should suffice,
Permission from the Pope that Walter take
Another wife, all for his people's sake.

I say, he bade that they should counterfeit
A papal bull, granting to him permission
His present wife and marchioness to set
Aside, as with the Pope's full dispensation,
To put a stop to the supposed dissension
Among his people. Thus declared the bull,
Which the Court granted and proclaimed in full.

The simple folk, and this no wonder was,
Believed the papal bull was right and true.
But when the tidings reached Griseld, alas,
I deem her heart was very full of woe.
But though cast down forever, even so

She was disposed in all humility
To bear of fortune the adversity.

She waited still his pleasure and his whim
To whom she had been given, heart and all,
Her very self, support of life and limb.
But since this story shortly I shall tell,
The Marquis meanwhile wrote a personal
And secret letter showing his intent
That to Bologna privately he sent.

The Earl, the ruler of Panicia, who
Was wedded to his sister, specially
He prayed that he should bring these children two
Home once again, in honor openly.
But one thing still he begged him utterly,
That no one know, though people might inquire,
Whose children they might be nor who their sire.

He was to say the maiden should be wed
Unto Saluzzo's Marquis very soon.
And as the Earl was asked, just so he did.
For on the day that they agreed upon
He took his way, with nobles many a one
In rich array, this maiden for to guide,
Her little brother riding at her side.

Now richly for her wedding was arrayed
This fresh young maid, decked out with jewels
    clear;
Her brother, seven years of age, beside
Was also nobly dressed for the affair.
And thus in high estate, with merry cheer
Off to Saluzzo set the company,
From day to day riding along the way.

Meanwhile the Marquis, on his wicked part,
To test his patient wife still more and more
E'en to the utter limit of her heart,
Fully to learn and every way be sure
That she were yet as steadfast as before,
Surrounded by his courtiers one day
Spoke to Griselda roughly in this way.

"Griselda, I have had delight, in sooth,
With you as wife, from all your righteousness,
As well from your obedience and truth,
But not from your estate or wealthiness.
Alas, I know in very truthfulness
That in great lordship, as I've well construed,
In sundry ways there is great servitude.

"I may not do as every plowman may.
My people call upon me now to take
Another wife and cry out day by day.
Therefore the Pope, their discontent to slake,
Consents that such a course I undertake.
And truly, therefore, this much I must say
To you. My new wife comes upon her way."

She answered him once more with sufferance.
"My lord," quoth she, "I know, and have alway,
Between your wealth and your magnificence
And my low state, no person can nor may
Make just comparison. It is no nay.
Unto my father gladly will I wend,
And dwell with him until my life shall end."

Thus with her father for a certain space
Griselda dwelt, in true obedience.
And neither in her words nor in her face

Before the folk betrayed her sentiments
Or showed that she had suffered grave offense.
And not a sign that she could still recall
Her high position offered she at all.

Now from Panicia the Earl hath come,
And soon the news was known to more and less.
And in the people's hearing, all and some,
'Twas known as well that a new marchioness
He had brought with him in such stateliness
That never was there seen with human eye
So noble an array in Lombardy.

The Marquis, who had planned and knew this all,
Before the Earl arrived, sent his commands
To poor Griselda in her cottage small.
And she with humble heart and countenance
And ne'er a thought of pride or arrogance
Came at his bidding, knelt upon her knee,
And did him reverence with modesty.

"Griselda," thus he spoke as if in play,
  "How does the beauty of my wife appear
  To you?" Said she, "Right well, my lord. I say
  I never saw a maid as she so fair.
  I pray God give prosperity to her;
  And hope as well that He to you will send
  Abundant blessing till your lives shall end.

"But one thing I beseech you, lord, this one:
  That you not trouble with your torturing
  This tender maid, as you to me have done.
  For she is sheltered in her nurturing
  More tenderly. And 'tis my fancying

She cannot bear so much adversity
As can a humble creature such as I."

Now when this Walter saw her sufferance,
Her quiet face, no malice there at all,
Though he had often done her great offense
And she remained as constant as a wall,
Keeping her gentle spirit over all,
The Marquis then must all his heart address
To think upon her wifely steadfastness.

"This is enough, Griselda mine," said he.
"Be thou no more ill-used, no more afraid.
I have thy faith and thy benignity,
As much as ever woman's was, assayed
In high estate as well as low, indeed.
Griseld," quoth he, "no other wife I have
Nor e'er have had, as God my soul may save.

"This is thy daughter, whom thou hast supposed
To be my wife. This other faithfully
Shall be my heir. No other I proposed.
Thou bore him as thy son in certainty.
I sent them to Bologna secretly.
Take them again. For now thou well mayst know
Thou hast lost neither of thy children two."

When this she heard, a-swooning down she fell
For sudden happiness. Then joyfully
Both her young children to her did she call
And in her arms, a-weeping piteously,
Embraced them both and kissed them tenderly
Like any mother. With her salty tears
She bathed their faces and their golden hairs.

The ladies of the court, when that they may,
Have taken her and to her chamber gone
And stripped her out of all her poor array
And in a cloth of gold that brightly shone—
A coronet with many a precious stone
Upon her head—into the hall they led her,
Where she received the honor that was owed
    her.

Full many a year in high prosperity
Lived Walter and Griseld in peace and rest.
He saw his daughter married splendidly
Unto a lord, one of the worthiest
Of Italy. And then in concord blest
His wife's old father at his court he kept
Until the spirit from his body crept.

His son succeeded to his seigniory
And lived in peace after his father's day.
In marriage also fortunate was he
(But his wife's patience he did not assay).
This world is not so strong, it is no nay,
As once it was in the old days of yore.
Now hearken what the author says therefore.

This tale is told, not that all women should
Follow Griselda in humility,
For that's impossible although they would.
The moral is that each in his degree
Should be as steady in adversity
As was Griselda. Petrarch so this tale
Hath written and composed in lofty style.

Phoebus and the Crow

The Manciple's Tale

Whan Phebus dwelled her in this erthe adoun,
As olde bokes maken mencioun,
He was the moste lusty bachiler
In al this world, and eek the beste archer. . . .

Chaucer included in his collection a number of stories illustrating various attitudes toward marriage. The story of Griselda has to do with a faithful wife who was a paragon of virtue. In the present tale, Chaucer uses an ancient folk fable to portray a marriage betrayed by the wife. The story of a talking bird punished for tattling is found all over the world. Chaucer took his version from the *Metamorphoses* of Ovid, a Latin poet who lived from 43 B.C. until 17 A.D.

> When Phoebus dwelt here in this earth adown,
> As ancient books have made his story known,
> He was the bravest knight at arms in all
> The world, and the best archer here as well.
> He slew Python the serpent as he lay
> Sleeping beneath the sun upon a day.
> And many another worthy noble deed
> With his true bow he wrought, as men may read.

He could play well on every instrument
And sing so well one heard a heaven-sent
Melody, when'er one heard his song.
The King of Thebes, indeed, King Amphion,
That with his singing raised the city wall,
Could never sing as Phoebus half so well.
What need I to describe his virtues so?

Now Phoebus had within his house a crow
Which in a cage he'd fostered many a day
And taught it speech, as men will teach a jay.
The crow was white as is the snow-white swan;
And counterfeit the speech of any man
He could, whene'er he wished to tell a tale.
Also, in all this world no nightingale
Knew how, by any hundred thousand way,
To sing so wondrous well and merrily.

Now Phoebus had within his house a wife
Whom he loved more than e'er he loved his life.
And night and day he wrought with diligence
To please her and to do her reverence;
Save only, if the truth I shall say plain,
Phoebus was jealous and would cage her in.
For he was loath deceivéd for to be.
And so is every man to some degree.

Take any bird and put it in a cage.
Then with thy best intent and fosterage
Nourish it tenderly with meat and drink
And all the dainties that thou mayest think,
And keep it just as cleanly as you may,
And though its cage with gold be e'er so gay,
Yet would this bird, by twenty thousand fold,

Rather in forest, which is rude and cold,
Go and eat worms and other wretchedness.
This bird will do his best in his distress
To fly out from his cage, if that he may;
His liberty a bird desireth aye.

Or take a cat and feed him well with milk
And tender flesh and make his couch of silk,
And let him see a mouse go by the wall—
Then out the window, milk and flesh and all
And every dainty that is in that house!
Such appetite he hath to eat a mouse.

This Phoebus now, for all his jollity,
Deceivéd was. Another man had she,
A man of little worth and small renown,
No match for Phoebus in comparison.

But so it was. When Phoebus off had gone,
His wife sent for her lover there anon.
The white crow saw them, but said ne'er a word.
And when in time came Phoebus, her own lord,
Then, "Cuckoo! Cuckoo! Cuckoo!" sang the crow.

"What, bird?" asked Phoebus. "What song singest
   thou?
Thou hast been wont so merrily to sing
That to my heart it brought a pleasuring
To hear thy voice. Alas! What song is this?"

"My lord," the crow said, "I sing not amiss.
Phoebus," he said, "for all thy worthiness,
For all thy beauty and thy gentleness,
For all thy singing and thy minstrelsy,

Enchanted is thy wife, blinded her eye
By one of little worth and small renown,
Not like to thee, but in comparison
A gnat unto a mountain, on my life.
But, with her leave, I've seen him love thy wife!"

What more do you desire? The crow has told
With sorry tokens and descriptions bold
How Phoebus' wife had acted wantonly
To bring to him great shame and villainy.
Then Phoebus thought his heart would burst in two.
He bent his bow and set an arrow so,
And in his wrath his wife he then hath slain.
This is the end, to speak it full and plain.
For sorrow then he broke his minstrelsy,
Both harp and lute, guitar and psaltery;
He broke as well his arrows and his bow.
And after that thus spake he to the crow.

"Traitor," he cried, "with tongue of scorpion!
Thou hast to my confusion brought me down.
Alas, that I was born! Would I were dead!
O lovely wife! O gem of wifelihood!
That were to me so faithful and so true,
Now liest thou dead with visage pale of hue
Full guiltlessly, that dare I say, iwiss!
O wretched hand to do so foul amiss!
O every man, beware of recklessness!
Believe you nothing without witnesses.
Smite none too soon, unless you know full why;
And seek advice, full well and soberly,
Ere that you do revenge or execution
On anyone in ire or suspicion.
Alas! For sorrow I myself shall slay!"

Then to the crow, "O evil thief," said he,
"Thee will I punish for thy wretched tale!
Once you could sing like any nightingale.
Now, wicked bird, you shall your song forego,
And all your feathers that were white as snow.
You and your offspring ever shall be black.
No more sweet melody or song you'll make,
But e'er cry out against the storm and rain,
In token that for you my wife is slain."

Then to the bird he started there anon
And pulled out the white feathers every one
And made him black, and took away his song,
And took his speech, and from the door he slung
Him to the devil, who his soul should take.
And this is why all crows must e'er be black!

The Rocks
of Brittany

The Franklin's Tale

In Armorik, that called is Britayne,
Ther was a knyght that loved and dide his payne
To serve a lady in his beste wyse;
And many a labour, many a great empryse
He for his lady wroghte, er she were wonne. . . .

This tale, like the one before it, is an ancient folk story
that turns up in many languages, ancient and modern.
The basic plot has to do with a lady who makes a promise containing what she thinks is an impossible condition.
Atalanta of Greek mythology, for instance, promises
to marry any man who can beat her on a foot race, a
feat that she believes cannot happen. Chaucer claims
to have taken his version from a "Breton lay," or ballad
from Brittany. As usual he gives it his own twist.

I have cut out much of the technical discussion of
magic and its relationship to astrology, which makes up
a large part of his account. Many people believed that
the movements of the heavenly bodies controlled human
fortunes. Others went so far as to think that the positions
of certain stars, and particularly of the moon, had their

effect on the laws of nature. An especially learned astrologer was thus able to perform feats of natural magic.

> In Armoric, sometimes called Brittany,
> There was a knight who loved and faithfully
> Served a fair lady in a noble wise.
> Many a labor, many an enterprise
> He wrought for her before that she was won,
> For she was of the fairest neath the sun.
> But at the last, for all his worthiness,
> She had such pity on his sore distress
> That graciously she fell into accord
> And took him for her husband and her lord.

> Now who can tell, unless he wedded be,
> The joy, the ease, and the prosperity
> There is between a husband and his wife?
> A year and more they led a blissful life
> Until the knight of whom I tell you thus
> Of Kerru, who was called Arveragus,
> Was moved to go and fight a year or two
> In England, which is oft called "Britain" too.
> He dwelt there for two years; the book says thus.

> Now I'll stop talking of Arveragus
> And speak to you of Dorigen, his wife,
> Who loved her husband as she loved her life.
> She mourned, she woke, she wailed, and she complained.
> Desire for his presence so constrained
> Her that this whole wide world she set at naught.
> Her friends, the ones who knew her heavy thought,
> Tried now to comfort her as best they may.
> They counseled her. They told her night and day

That without cause she slew herself, alas!
They gave her every solace that there was.

And so it happened in the morningtide
Into a garden that was close beside
They went to frolic all the livelong day.
And this was on the sixth morning of May,
When May had painted with his gentle showers
This garden full of greenery and flowers.
The fragrant odor and the pleasant sight
Would make the heart of anyone full light
That e'er was born, unless great heaviness
Or too great sorrow held it in distress—
This garden had such worth and elegance.
And after dinner there they went to dance
And sing as well, save Dorigen alone,
Who ever in her sorrow made her moan.

Now in the dance among the other men
Appeared a squire before Dorigen
That fresher was, of handsomer array,
In my opinion, than the month of May.
And, shortly if the truth I were to tell,
Unknown, unguessed by Dorigen at all,
This lusty squire, slave to Venus sworn,
Who by the name Aurelius was known,
Had loved her best of any lady fair,
As was his fortune, two long years or more.
For he was hopeless; nothing dared he say,
Save in his songs a little might he cry
His woe as in a general complaint.
He loved, but she did not, was his lament.
Of such a theme he fashioned many lays,
Songs and complaints, roundels and virilays.

But Dorigen knew naught of his intent.
It happened, nonetheless, before they went,
Because he'd been a neighbor long before,
They fell to speaking. Forward more and more
Unto his purpose drove Aurelius.
And when he saw the chance, he ventured thus:

"Madame," quoth he, "by God that hath us made,
If I could know that it would make you glad,
I'd wish that on the day Arveragus
Went out to sea that I, Aurelius,
Had gone too, never to come home again,
For well I know my service is in vain.
My guerdon is the breaking of my heart.
Madame, have pity on my sorrow's smart,
For with a word ye may me slay or save.
Here at your feet God would I had my grave!
I have as now no leisure more to say.
Have mercy, sweet, or you will make me die."

She turned to look upon Aurelius.
"Is this your will?" said she. "And say'st thee thus?
Not once have I suspected what you meant!
But now, sir, that I know your true intent,
I say by God that gave me soul and life
That I shall never be a faithless wife
In word or deed, so long as I have wit.
I will be his to whom that I am knit.
Take this for final answer, sir, from me."
But afterwards in play thus added she:

"Aurelius," she said, "by God above,
Still would I grant that I would be your love,
Since I see you complain so piteously.

That day when from the coast of Brittany
You take out all the rocks, each stone by stone,
So they no longer hinder ships to run;
I say, when ye have made the coast so clean
Of rocks and stones that none can there be seen,
Then will I love you best of any man.
Have here my word in all that e'er I can."

"Is there no other grace in you?" asked he.

"No, by the Lord," she said, "that makéd me.
For well I know this never shall betide.
Now let these follies from your reason slide."

Aurelius was sad when this he heard,
And with a grieving heart he gave his word.
"Madame," said he. "This is impossible.
Now comes my death, sudden and horrible."
And with this word he turned away again.

Then came of her companions many a one
And thereupon began their games anew
Until the shining sun had lost his hue.

Aurelius felt his heart was growing cold.
Up to heaven then his hands he held,
And on his bare knees now he set him down
And in his raving made this orison.
He said, "Apollo, lord and governor
Of every plant and herb and tree and flower,
Now, as thy mansion changeth, low or high,
Lord Phoebus, cast thy merciable eye
Upon me, wretch Aurelius, here forlorn.
Lo, lord, my lady hath my death y-sworn.

"Your blesséd sister, fair and bright Lucine,
Is of the sea the goddess and the queen.
Therefore, Lord Phoebus, this is my request.
Perform this wonder, or my heart will burst.
Pray her so very great a flood to bring
That fathoms five at least it overspring
The highest cliff that edges Brittany,
And let this flood endure two years. Then I
In certainty to Dorigen may say,
'Now keep your word. The rocks are gone away!'

"Thy shrine at Delphi barefoot will I seek.
Lord Phoebus, see the tears upon my cheek,
And on my pain have some compassion soon."
And with that word he fell down in a swoon,
And for a long time in a trance he lay.

His brother, who knew all his agony,
Hath found him, and to bed he hath him brought.
Thus hopeless in this torment, thus distraught,
Let I this woeful squire, Aurelius, lie.
Choose ye for me whether he live or die.

Arveragus, with tribute and with honor
For him that was of chivalry the flower,
Came home again with other worthy men.
O blesséd art thou now, Dame Dorigen!
Thou hast thy lusty husband in thine arms,
The hearty knight, the worthy man-at-arms.

In languor and in torment furious
For two years lay the wretch Aurelius
Ere on the earth his foot he might set down.
Of comfort in this time he had but none
Save from his brother, he that was a clerk.

He knew of all this woe, of all this work,
For to no other creature certainly
Aurelius dared a word of it to say.

This clerk recalled that once while he had been
At Orleans, in his studies he had seen
A book of natural magic his confrere,
Who of the law was then a bachelor,
Though he was there to learn another craft,
In private on his reading desk had left.
This book spoke much of all the operations
Touching upon the eight and twenty mansions
That are the moon's, and such absurdity
As in our day is thought not worth a fly.
Now when this book came to this clerk's recall,
For joy his heart began to dance withal;
And to himself he said delightedly,
"My brother shall be cured, and speedily.

"In Orleans if I could some fellow find
Who hath the mansions of the moon in mind,
Or other magic, nature's laws above,
He well might help my brother have his love,
For with a magic show a clerk can make
It seem in human sight that all the black
Rocks of the Breton coast have been destroyed,
And on the waves ships may unhindered ride,
And in such form endure a day or two.
My brother would be cured of all his woe.
Then must she keep the promise that she made,
Or else he can bring shame to her," he said.

Why should I make a longer tale of this?
Unto his brother's bed he came, iwiss,

And such advice he gave, that he should go
To Orleans. He started up, and so
Upon his way Aurelius doth fare
In hope to be relieved of all his care.

When they had come almost to that cit́y
Except for just a furlong two or three,
A young clerk wandering by himself they met
Who in the Latin tongue made his salute.
And after that he said a wondrous thing.
"I know," quoth he, "the hopes that here you bring."
And ere a single foot they further went,
He told them all that was in their intent.

Now off his horse Aurelius leaped down,
And forth with this magician is he gone.
This clerk hath shown, ere they had supper there,
Forests and wooded parks full of wild deer.
There saw Aurelius harts with antlers high,
The greatest ever seen with human eye.
And after this the clerk made a display.
He showed his lady at a dance, where he
Himself was dancing with her, so he thought.
And when this master who this magic wrought
Saw it was time, he clapped his hands anon.
And, farewell! All the revels there were gone.

After their supper they fell bargaining
About the sum the master's work should bring
If he removed the rocks from Brittany,
From the Gironde unto the Seine, pardee.
He made objections, swore as God him save,
Less than a thousand pounds he would not have,
Nor was he even glad to work for this.

Aurelius, whose heart was mad for bliss,
Answered him thus. "Fie on a thousand pound!
This whole wide world, which many say is round.
I'd give it all, if I were lord of it.
This bargain is full driven. We are knit!"

Upon the morrow when that it was day
To Brittany they took the shortest way,
Aurelius with the master at his side,
And they dismounted where he would abide.
And this was, as from old books I remember,
The cold and frosty season of December.
Phoebus, I dare well say, like pewter shone.
The bitter frosts, and with them sleet and rain,
Destroyéd have the green in every yard.
Janus sits by the fire with double beard
And drinketh from his bugle horn the wine.
Before him stands the flesh of tuskéd swine,
And "Noel!" cryeth every lusty man.

Aurelius, in every way he can,
Does to the clerk, the master, reverence,
And prays him now to work with diligence
To bring an end to all his pain and smart,
Or with a sword he vows to slit his heart.

The clerk has so much pity for the man
That night and day he speeds as best he can.
His tables of Toledo forth he brought,
Full well corrected, for he lacked in naught.
He knew the moon's arising very well
And in whose face and term, and every deal.
He knew as well the proper lunar mansion

Accordant with his present operation,
As heathen folk believed in ancient days.
Therefore he made no useless long delays,
But through his magic in a week or two
It seemed that all the rocks were made to go.

Aurelius, who still in anguish is
If he will have his love or fare amiss,
Waits night and day to see this miracle.
And when he knows there is no obstacle,
That all the rocks are vanished, every one,
Down at the master's feet he falls anon
And says, "I, woeful wretch, Aurelius,
Thank you, my lord, and you, O bounteous
Venus, who heal me of my sorrows cold."

He to the temple now his way doth hold,
There where he knew he should his lady see.
And when he saw the time was right, then he
With fearful heart and with full humble cheer
Hath greeted there his sovereign lady dear.

"My proper lady," quoth this woeful man,
  "Whom I most fear and love the best I can,
  You know right well what you have promised me
  When in my hand your troth then plighted ye
  To love me best, God knows you said it so,
  Although I am unworthy that you do.
  Now I have done as you commanded me.
  And if you will vouchsafe, you may go see.
  Do as you wish, but keep your pledge in mind,
  For quick or dead, right there ye shall me find.
  In you it lies to let me live, or slay.
  But well I wot, the rocks are gone away!"

He took his leave, and she astonished stood.
In all her face was ne'er a drop of blood.
She never could have thought of such a trap.
"Alas!" quoth she, "that ever this should hap.
I never dreamed the possibility
That such a monstrous marvel there could be.
It is against the processes of nature!"
And home she went again, a sorry creature.

For fear she scarcely now could move or go.
She wept and wailed throughout a day or two
And swooned, it was a pity for to see.
But why this was, to none confided she,
For off once more had gone Arveragus.
But to herself she spake and sorrowed thus.
"Alas," she said, "to Fortune I complain
That wraps me, all unwary, in her chain,
Which to escape I know no other succor
Save only death; if otherwise, dishonor.
One or another of these I must choose.
But, nonetheless, still had I liefer lose
My life than on my body bear a shame
Or know that I am false or lose my name."

Thus sorrowed Dorigen a day or two,
Intending ever to her death to go,
But, nonetheless, anon, on the third night,
Home came Arveragus, that worthy knight.
He asked her why she wept so very sore.
And she began to weep again the more.

"Alas," she cried, "that ever I was born!
Thus have I said," quoth she. "Thus have I sworn."
She told him all that you have heard before;
I need rehearse it here for you no more.

This husband in good cheer and friendly wise
Answered and said as I shall you devise.
"Is there aught else, my Dorigen, but this?"

"Nay, nay," quoth she, "God help me so, iwiss!
This is too much, although it be God's will."

"Yea, wife," he said, "let sleep that which is still.
All may indeed be well, even today.
But you must keep your promise, by my fay!
May God above have mercy upon me!
I would much liefer stabbéd for to be,
Here by the love which I for you do have,
Than you should fail to keep the pledge you gave.
Truth is the highest good a man may keep."
But at this word he burst aloud to weep
And said, "I you forbid on pain of death
That ever while you cherish life or breath
To any one you speak of this affair.
As best I may, my sorrow I shall bear."

Then forth he called a squire and a maid.
"Go forth at once with Dorigen," he said.
"Bring her to such and such a place anon."

They took their leave and on their way were gone,
But they knew not the reason that she went,
For he would tell no one of his intent.

The squire who was called Aurelius,
Who after Dorigen was amorous,
As if by chance now happened her to meet
Within the town, right in a busy street,
As she was bound to go the shortest way
To that same garden, there her debt to pay.

And he was going to the garden, too,
For well he spied whenever she would go
Out of her house to any other place.
And thus they met by chance, or else by grace;
And he saluted her with glad intent
And asked of her then whitherward she went.

She answered him, as if she were half mad.
"Unto the garden, as my husband bade,
My promise for to keep. Alas! Alas!"

Aurelius now wondered at the case,
And in his heart had pity and compassion
On her and on her woeful lamentation,
And on Arveragus, the worthy knight,
Who bade her keep her word, for this was right,
So loath was he his wife should break her troth.
And in his heart Aurelius felt great ruth,
For which in a few words he answered thus:

"Madame, say to your lord, Arveragus,
 That since I see how great his gentleness
 To you, and also see your sore distress,
 I had much rather ever suffer woe
 Than to betray the love betwixt you two.
 I here release you, madame, to your hand,
 Free of your every pledge and every bond.
 My troth I plight. I grant you full reprieve
 Of your behest. And here I take my leave
 Of you, the truest and most faithful wife
 That ever yet I knew in all my life.
 Thus can a squire do a gentle deed
 As well as a knight can," Aurelius said.

She thanketh him upon her knees all bare,
And home unto her husband doth she fare.
She tells him all that you have heard me tell.
You may be certain that it pleased him well.

Arveragus and Dorigen his wife
In sovereign bliss led their remaining life.
No quarrel or anger ever came between.
He cherished her as though she were a queen,
And she to him was true forevermore.
Of these two folk you'll hear of me no more.

Aurelius, his cause now all forlorn,
Curseth the time that ever he was born.
"Alas," quoth he, "that ever I have told
That I would pay a thousand pounds of gold
Unto this clerk! Whatever shall I do?
'Tis utter ruin I am coming to!
My heritage indeed I needs must sell
And be a beggar. Here I may not dwell
To shame all of my kindred in this place,
Unless of him I get a better grace."

With sorry heart he goeth to his chest
And bringeth gold unto the alchemist,
The value of five hundred pounds, I guess,
And him beseecheth of his gentleness
To grant more days in which to pay the rest
And saith, "Sir clerk, I dare well make a boast
In honor I have never faltered yet.
My debt to you will certainly be quit,
No matter in what manner I may fare,
If I go begging in my kirtle bare.
But would ye vouchsafe on security

To let me have two years or even three,
Then I were fortunate. Else, I must sell
My heritage. There is no more to tell."

The clerk spoke plainly to Aurelius
When he had heard these words and answered thus:
"Have I not kept my covenant to thee?"

"Yea, certain, well and faithfully," quoth he.

"Hast thou not had thy lady by thy side?"

"Nay, no!" quoth he, and sorrowfully he sighed.

"What was the reason? Tell me if you can."

Aurelius his sad tale anon began
And told him all, as you have heard before.
There is no need that I rehearse it more.

Then the magician answered, "My dear brother,
Each of you acted nobly to the other.
Thou art a squire, and he is a knight.
But God forbid, in all His blesséd might,
If a clerk could not do a noble deed
As well as any one of you," he said.

"Sir, I release you from your thousand pound,
As if right now you'd risen from the ground
And never until now laid eyes on me.
For, sir, no penny will I take from thee
For all my labor or for all my skill.
For my provisioning you have paid well.
That is enough. Now, farewell! Have good day!"
He took his horse and went upon his way.

Lordings, this question would I ask you now.
Which of them was most generous, think you?
Now tell me this, ere further you shall wend.
I'll say no more. My tale is at an end.

The Ballad
of Sir Thopas

Chaucer's Tale

Listeth, lordes, in good entent,
And I wol telle verrayment
* Of mirthe and of solas;*
Al of a knyght was fair and gent
In bataille and in tourneyment,
* His name was sir Thopas.*

Late in the journey the Host asks Geoffrey to tell a story. The latter replies that he knows only one, a rhymed tale about a knight, but he will be glad to tell that. Then he proceeds to recite a parody of the then popular romantic ballads about knights and their adventures with giants and fairy queens. In deadpan fashion, Chaucer makes fun not only of these ballads but of the bourgeois knights of his day. (See the preface to the Knight in "The Prologue.") He piles up detail after detail of nonsense. The name Thopas, for example, means topaz, a jewel, but only a semiprecious one. His hero comes from Poperinghe, a weaving center in Flanders, whose population was solidly middle class. Sir Thopas' clothing, from his cordwain (Cordovan leather) shoes to his linen underwear, is typical of that of a

well-to-do merchant. In his adventure with the giant
Olifant, whose name, by the way, means elephant, Sir
Thopas has apparently neglected to put on his armor.
As a result, he has to go home to get dressed before he
can battle with his foe. There are many of these little
digs.

Unfortunately, the Host thinks that Geoffrey's tale is
dull and asks him to stop. Now we shall never know
the outcome of the battle between the doughty knight
and the three-headed giant. Geoffrey, alas, launches in-
stead into a *really* dull tale about a man named Melibeus,
which is not included here.

> Listen, lords, in good intent,
> And I shall tell, with your consent,
>> Of mirth, of jest, of game,
> About a knight of gentle bent
> In battle and in tournament.
>> Sir Thopas was his name.
>
> In a far country born was he,
> In Flanders all across the sea.
>> Poperinghe was the place.
> His father was a man full free,
> And of that country lord was he,
>> As it was heaven's grace.
>
> Sir Thopas was a doughty swain.
> White was his face as pandemain;
>> His lips were red as rose;
> His cheeks were flushed with scarlet stain,
> And I can tell you it was plain
>> He had a seemly nose.

His hair, his beard was saffron tone
That to his girdle reached adown.
        His shoes were fine cordwain.
His hose of Bruges cloth were brown.
His mantle was of ciclatoun
        Which cost full many a jane.

And he could hunt the running deer
And ride a-hawking anywhere,
        His goshawk on his hand.
He was as well an archer fair.
At wrestling no one was his peer
        Where any ram should stand.

Full many a maiden in her bower
Yearned for him as paramour
        When she should be asleep.
But he was chaste, no evil-doer,
And sweet as is the bramble flower
        That beareth the red hip.

It so befell that on a day
Forsooth, as tell it you I may,
        Sir Thopas went to ride.
He leapt upon his steed of gray,
And in his hand a lancegay,
        A long sword at his side.

Throughout a wood he made his quest
Wherein were many a savage beast,
        Indeed, the buck and hare;
And as he trotted north and east,
I tell it you, to him almost
        Befell a sorry care.

There flourished herbs both great and small,
The licorice and cetewale
    And many a gillyflower,
And nutmeg for to put in ale,
Whether it be fresh or stale,
    Or in a chest or bower.

The birds they sang, it is no nay,
The sparrow hawk, the popinjay,
    That joy it was to hear.
The thrustlecock made eke his lay,
And the wood pigeon on the spray,
    She sang full loud and clear.

Sir Thopas fell in reverie,
There where he heard the thrustle cry,
    And rode as he were mad.
He spurred his worthy steed, till he
So sweated you might wring him dry.
    His sides were wet with blood.

Sir Thopas also weary was
From racing through the rustling grass.
    So fierce his heart did beat
That down he laid him in that place
To give his steed a little peace,
    Also to let him eat.

"Oh, *Benedic'té*, Saint Marie!
Why doth this love so trouble me
    And fetter me so sore?
I dreaméd all the night, pardee,
An elf-queen shall my lover be,
    My mistress and my dear.

"An elf-queen will I love, iwiss,
For in this world no woman is
    Worthy to be my own.
All other women I forsake,
And to an elf-queen I'll me take
    By dale and eke by down."

Upon his steed he climbed again
And cantered over stile and stone
    An elf-queen to espy,
Till he so long had ridden and gone
That finally he came upon
    The land of Faéry
        So wild;
For in that country there was none
Who dared to him to ride or run,
    Neither wife nor child,

Until there came a giant gaunt;
His title was Sir Olifant,
    A fearful man indeed.
He said, "Sir Knight, by Termagaunt,
Unless thou hasten from my haunt,
    At once I'll slay thy steed
        With my mace.
Know you, the Queen of Faéry
With harp and pipe and symphony
    Is dwelling in this place."

The Knight said, "*Benedicité!*
Tomorrow will I meet with thee
    When I've my armor here.
And yet I hope, upon my fay,
That thou shalt with this lancegay

Pay for this full dear.
        Thy brain
Shall I shatter, if I may,
Ere it be fully prime of day,
        For here thou shalt be slain."

Sir Thopas drew aback full fast,
For now the giant at him cast
        Stones out of a sling.
But Thopas hath escaped apace,
And it was all through heaven's grace
        And through his scurrying.

Yet listen, lordings, to my tale
Merrier than the nightingale,
        For I shall tell anon
How Thopas hastened to his hall
And, riding over hill and dale,
        Is come again to town.

His merry men commanded he
To make for him both game and glee,
        For needs must be to fight
A giant who of heads had three,
All for the love and jollity
        Of her who shone full bright.

They fetched him first the fragrant mead
And wine in bowl of maplewood
        With many a fragrant spice,
And dainty bits of gingerbread
And licorice and cumin seed
        And sugar of great price.

Next to his white skin he wore,
Of cloth of linen fine and clear,
    His breeches and his shirt.
And next his shirt an aketon,
And over that an habergeon
    For to protect his heart.

And over that a fine hauberk
That was wrought all of Jewish work,
    Full strong it was with plate;
And over that his armor-coat—
As lily flower it was white—
    In which he should debate.

His shield was all of gold so red.
Upon it was a wild boar's head,
    A carbuncle beside;
And there he swore by ale and bread
How that the giant "shall be dead,
    Betide what may betide."

His leggings were of quirboilly.
His scabbard was of ivory,
    His helm of latten bright.
His saddle was of rewel-bone.
His bridle like the sunlight shone
    Or like the moon's clear light.

His spear was of the cypress wood
That never peace but war doth bode.
    Its head was sharply ground.
His steed was all of dapple gray;
It went an-ambling on its way
    Full softly through the land.

His sturdy steed he then bestrode,
And forth upon his way he rode,
    Like sparklet from a flame.
Upon his crest he bore a tower
And in it stuck a lily flower.
    God shield his course from shame!

He was a knight adventurous.
He would not sleep in any house,
    But lay out in his hood,
His helm his pillow, while his steed
Was tethered him beside and fed
    On grasses fine and good.

He drank the water of the well
As did the knight, Sir Percival,
    So worthy in his weeds,
Till on a day—

Here the Host asks Chaucer to stop this Tale of
Thopas.

The Story
of Constance

The Tale of the Man of Law

In Surrie whylom dwelte a companye
Of chapmen riche, and therto sadde and trewe,
That wyde-wher senten her spycerye,
Clothes of gold, and satins riche of hewe;
Hir chaffar was so thrifty and so newe
That every wight hath deyntee to chaffare
With hem, and eek to sellen hem hir ware.

The story of Constance, which Chaucer probably
picked up from an Anglo-Norman chronicle of the
early fourteenth century, belongs to a group of folk
tales about abused wives, as does the story of Griselda.
Variants of these stories turn up in Oriental as well as
European folklore—and on our own TV screens. In
this particular version, the poor lady has trouble with
her two mothers-in-law. You will read about only one
of them, for the account is cut off here in the middle.
During the latter half of the tale, the second wicked
old woman sets the poor girl adrift on the ocean, just
as the first had done. This time, Constance and her
baby son Maurice drift for years until she is rescued
and eventually reunited with her husband and her father.

The historic allusions in the tale are vague. A Tiberius who had a daughter Constantina was a Roman Emperor, but he was Emperor of the *Eastern* Roman Empire during the sixth century A.D. His son-in-law, not his grandson, Mauritius, followed him as Emperor in Constantinople.

In Syria once dwelt a company
Of merchants, rich and serious and true.
To other lands they sent their spicery,
Their cloth of gold and satins rich of hue.
The goods they had were thrifty and so new
That everyone was pleased with them to trade,
To buy their wares and sell the wares he had.

These merchants made their sojourn in the town
Of Rome awhile, for their employment there.
As it befell, the excellent renown
Of Constance, daughter of the Emperor,
Was spread abroad by all who met them there
Unto these Syrian merchants in such wise
From day to day as I shall you advise.

This was the common voice of every man.
"Our Emperor of Rome, may God him bless,
Hath a fair daughter. Since the world began,
To tell you of her worth and loveliness,
Another such as she there never was.
I pray that God in honor her sustain
And wish she were of all the West the queen."

Now it befell these merchants stood in grace
With him who was the Sultan of Syrie,
And when they came from any foreign place,
He would, in token of his courtesy,

Make them good cheer, and also he would ply
These men with questions, that he might have word
Of any wonders they had seen or heard.

Thus among other things especially
The merchants told the Sultan of Constánce
In such particular, so earnestly,
That he was seized by sudden exigence
To have her for himself. This Syrian prince
Declared his only wish, his only need,
Was that he love her while his life abide.

The Sultan for his privy council sent
And, shortly in this matter for to pace,
He hath to them declared his full intent
And told them thus: unless he had the grace
To wed this Constance in a little space,
Then he would lose his life. He charged them hie
To find for his distress the remedy.

But difficulties great therein saw they
For the good reason, here to speak it plain,
That there was such a vast diversity
Between the countries' laws, that they have seen,
They trow, no Christian ruler would be fain
To let his daughter marry in the code
Of law Mahomet hath received from God.

He answered them, "Rather than that I lose
Constance, I will be christened, nonetheless.
I must be hers; no other way I choose.
I pray you hold your arguments in peace.
Now save my life, and be no way remiss
To seek her who hath for my ills the cure,
For in this woe I may not long endure."

And now the Sultan and his baronage
And all his vassal knights shall christened be.
And he shall have Constance in marriáge,
With gold, I know not in what quantity,
But it was found sufficient surety.
The same accord was sworn on either side.
Now Constance, God Almighty be thy guide.

At last the day came for her journeying.
I say the woeful fatal day was come.
Now might there be no longer tarrying,
But forward they must press, both all and some.
Constance, who was with sorrow overcome,
Full pale arose and readied her to wend,
For well she saw there was no other end.

To ship was brought this woeful lovely maid
Full solemnly, with pomp and circumstance.
"Now Jesus Christ be with you all," she said.
There was no more but, "Farewell, fair Constánce."
She forced herself to hold good countenance.
And forth I let her journey on the water
While I turn once again to other matter.

The mother of the Sultan, well of vices,
Hath learned about her son's declared intent
That he would stop the ancient sacrifices.
Then for her council suddenly she sent.
And when they came to hearken what she meant,
And when together gathered were the folk,
She set her down and thus to them she spoke.

"My lords," said she, "you know, each, every one,
  My son is now determined to forbid
  The holy laws, those giv'n in the Koran

Unto Mahomet, messenger of God.
But this avowal make I unto God.
The life shall sooner from my body start
Than shall Mahomet's law go from my heart.

"What shall this new law bring to you and me
But thralldom for our bodies and regret?
And afterwards in hell we'll ever be,
For we denied our prophet, Mahomét?
But, noble lords, some hope is left us yet.
If you to my proposal here will swear,
I shall hold us in safety ever more.

"We first shall feign the Christian law to take.
Cold water shall not grieve us but a mite.
And I shall such a feast and revel make
It shall indeed the Sultan well requite,
For though his wife be christened ne'er so white,
She shall have need to wash away the red,
Though she a fount of water with her led."

At last the Christian folk arrived to land
In Syria with a great solemn rout.
The Sultan now a messenger doth send
To her, his dame, and nobles all about
And said his wife was coming, without doubt,
And begged them for to ride to meet the Queen
And thus the honor of the realm sustain.

Great was the press, and rich was the array
Of Syrians and Romans meeting there.
The mother of the Sultan, rich and gay,
Receiveth Constance with a happy cheer
As any mother might her daughter dear.

Now to the Sultan's palace there beside
At gentle pace with dignity they ride.

At last the time came. The old Sultaness
Ordainéd hath the feast of which I told.
And to the revels Christian folk then press
In multitudes, yea, both the young and old.
Here they might feast and royalty behold,
With dainties more than I can here disclose.
But all too dear they bought them ere they rose.

For shortly for to tell you in a word,
The Sultan and the Christians every one,
They were attacked and murdered at the board,
Except for Constance, save for her alone.
This evil Sultaness, this curséd crone,
Hath with her rascals done a curséd deed,
For she herself would all the country lead.

Among the Christian Syrians was none
Who in the council of the Sultan sat
But ere he could defend himself was slain.
And Constance they have seized upon the spot
And in a ship without a rudder set
And bade her learn to sail across the sea
Away from Syria home to Italy.

The gold and treasure that she thither led
And, truth to say, of food sufficiency
They gave to her and all the clothes she had,
And forth she saileth in the salty sea.
O Constance, lady of benignity,
O dearest daughter of the Emperor,
He that is Lord of Fortune be thine oar!

Though at the first she was not slain, Who now
Kept her from drowning in the salty sea?
And Who kept Jonah in the fish's maw
Till he was spouted up at Nineveh?
Well may you know it was no one but He
Who kept the Hebrew folk from getting wet
When through the sea they passed upon dry feet.

She drifted forth into the ocean stream
Across our stormy sea, till at the last
Under a castle that I cannot name
Far in Northumberland Constance was cast.
And in the sand the ship was stuck so fast
That thence it would not budge, for all the tide.
The will of Christ was that she should abide.

The castle's constable climbed down to shore
To see this wreck. Throughout the ship he sought
And found this weary woman full of care,
And to the land this woman he hath brought.
In her own language mercy she besought,
But what she was, indeed, she would not say
Through foul or fair, even though she should die.

The constable and Hermengild his wife
Were pagans, as were all the people there.
But Hermengild loved Constance as her life,
And Constance hath for so long sojourned there
With orisons and many a bitter tear
That Jesus hath converted through His grace
Dame Hermengild, the mistress of that place.

Satan, who ever waiteth to beguile
Us here on earth, saw Constance's perfection
And cast about how he might do her ill.

He made a young knight there conceive a passion,
Love her so hot and with such foul affection
That verily he thought he should expire
Unless he have of her his great desire.

He wooed her, but his suit availeth naught,
For she would not be led in any way.
Then, out of malice, he contrived a plot
To see that she a shameful death should die.
Until the constable had gone away,
He waited, and upon a night he crept
Into Hermengild's chamber as she slept.

Weary, exhausted from her constant prayer,
Now Constance sleeps, and Hermengild also.
This false knight, through the guile of Lucifer,
Now stealthily unto the bed doth go.
He cuts the throat of Hermengild in two,
Then beside Constance lays his bloody knife
And goes his way. Now may he rue his life!

Thereon the constable came home again,
With him King Aella of Northumberland.
He saw his wife, so pitifully slain,
For which full oft he wept and wrung his hand.
And in the bed the bloody knife he found
Beside Dame Constance. Ah, what could she say?
For very woe her wits were gone away.

She set her on her knees, and thus she said:
"Immortal God, Thou Who hast saved Susannah
From reckless blame, and Thou, merciful maid,
Mary, I mean, the daughter of Saint Anna,
Before whose Child the angels sing Hosanna,
If I be guiltless of this felony,
My succor be, for otherwise I die."

King Aella had so great compassion then,
As gentle heart is filled with sympathy,
That from his eyes the water ran adown.
"Now hastily go, fetch a book," quoth he,
"And if this knight will swear thereon how she
This woman slew, with justice then we shall
Advise on whom the punishment shall fall."

A British book of the Evangelist
Was fetched. And the young knight swore there-
upon
That she was guilty. Suddenly was thrust
A hand which smote him on the collarbone,
And down he fell at once, still as a stone,
And in a trice his eyes burst from his face
In sight of everybody in the place.

A voice was heard by all the people there
Which said, "Thou slanderest a guiltless maid,
The daughter of the church, in holy ear.
This thou hast done!" The awful voice hath said.
Aghast to hear this marvel was the crowd.
Amazéd there they stood, dumb every one,
For fear of the Lord's wrath, save her alone.

Great was the penitence and great the fear
Of them that had suspected wrongfully
This simple innocent, this Constance here.
And through this miracle, eventually,
And interceding prayers from Constance, yea,
The King, with many another in that place,
Hath been converted, thanks to Jesus' grace.

The faithless knight was slain for his untruth
At the command of Aella hastily,

But Constance still had pity for his death.
And after this Lord Jesus mercifully
Made Aella marry with full dignity
This holy maid who hath so bright a sheen.
And thus was Constance once more made a Queen.

The Wily
Alchemist

The Canon's Yeoman's Tale

This false chanoun cam up-on a day
Unto this preestes chambre, wher he lay,
Biseching him to lene him a certeyn
Of gold, and he wolde quyte it him ageyn. . . .

When the Pilgrims approach Boughton-under-Blee close to Canterbury, they are overtaken by a pair of sweating horsemen. These turn out to be a canon and his servant, or yeoman. They explain that they have ridden to catch up with the party because they enjoy good company. The Yeoman boasts to the Host of his master's prowess as an alchemist. The latter, he claims, can turn the road to pure gold. The Host, looking at the Canon's dingy surplice, expresses his doubts. Thereupon the Yeoman begins a very frank discussion of all the dishonest tricks employed by his master. After the Canon flees in embarrassment, the Yeoman regales his new companions with a story about a deceitful canon-alchemist, who, he says, is not his master. A canon, incidentally, is a clergyman, a member of a religious order, usually engaged in the service of a cathedral.

So far as we know, this story is original. Some scholars think that Chaucer wrote it out of resentment at having been gulled by an alchemist. He describes the typical procedures in enough detail to have dabbled in the experiments himself. Many intelligent people of the time believed it was possible to turn base metals into gold. It is hard to believe, however, that Chaucer would have been gullible. Too many of his references to alchemy are skeptical, to say the least.

A sly, false-hearted canon came one day
Unto the chamber where a young priest lay,
Beseeching him to lend him just a bit
Of gold, and he would soon repay the debt.
"Lend me a mark," he said, "for days but three,
And on the third day I shall bring it thee.
And should you find me false, indeed, you may
Then hang me by the neck another day."

The priest gave him a mark of gold, and then
The canon thanked him oft, and thereupon
He took his leave and went upon his way.
He brought the money on the proper day,
And to the priest he gave the gold again,
At which the priest was wondrous glad and fain.

"Surely," he said," it is a joy to me
To lend a man a mark, or two or three,
Or anything that is in my possession,
When he is thus so true to his condition
That in no way he fails to meet his day.
To such a man I never can say nay."

"What!" cried the canon. "Should I be untrue?
Nay, that were something strange, completely new!
Faith is the thing that I shall ever keep

Until the very day that I shall creep
Into my grave. If else, why, God forbid!
Believe this just as surely as the Creed!
And, sir," he said, "now, very privately,
Since you have been so friendly unto me
And shown to me so great a gentleness,
In some way to repay your kindliness
I here will show you, and, if you desire,
I'll teach you, too, the method and the manner
In which I work the craft of alchemy.
Take heed, good sir, you shall see with your eye
That I shall work a marvel ere I go."

"Yea," cried the priest, "indeed, and will you so?
Do this, I pray you, sir, most heartily."

"At your command," the canon said, "pardee!"

The priest knew not at all with whom he dealt;
And of the harm to come he nothing felt.
O silly priest! O simple innocent!
Thine avarice shall bring thy punishment!

"Sir," said the canon, "let your servant go
For quicksilver, that we may have it now,
And let him bring us ounces two or three.
And when he brings them back, then you will see
A wondrous thing which you ne'er saw ere this."

"Sir," said the priest, "it shall be done apace."
He bade his knave the mercury to fetch.
All ready at his bidding was the wretch
And went him forth and came back once again
With the quicksilver, thus to tell it plain,
And to the canon brought these ounces three.

The canon laid them down full carefully
And bade the knave bring coals to build a fire
That he might start to work the priest's desire.

The coals were fetched as soon as possible.
The wily canon took a crucible
Out from his cloak and showed it to the priest.
"This instrument," he said, "which here thou seest,
Take in thine hand, and thyself put therein
Of quicksilver an ounce. And thus begin,
In heaven's name, to be an alchemist.
There are but few to whom I have the list
To show my science, even such as this.
For you shall see with your own eyes, iwiss,
That this quicksilver I shall mortify,
Here in your sight right now, without a lie,
And make it into silver good and fine
As any there is in your purse or mine.
Send your man off, and let him stay without,
And shut the door while we two are about
Our secret business, that no one espy
The work we do here at this alchemy."
Just as he bade, all was fulfilled in deed.
The knave was ordered from the room with speed.
His master shut the door again, and so
Now to their labors eagerly they go.

The priest, in answer to the canon's will,
Upon the fire set the crucible
And blew the fire, busied him full fast.
The cursèd canon in the fire cast
A powder, I know not of what it was—
Perhaps 'twas made of chalk, perhaps of glass,
Or something else which was not worth a fly—

To satisfy the priest, and bade him hie
To heap the burning coals up high above
The crucible. "In token of my love,"
Said the sly canon, "with thine own hands two
Thou shalt do everything that here we do."

"*Grand merci!*" said the priest and was full glad.
He heaped the coals up as the canon bade.
While he was busy thus, this evil wretch,
This canon false (may the foul Fiend him fetch!)
Out of his bosom took a wooden coal
In which full subtly had been bored a hole
(An ounce of silver had been poured within)
Plugged up with wax to hold the silver in.

Now, pay attention, sirs, for God's own love!
He took this coal of which I spoke above
And in his hand he bore it secretly.
And while the priest continued busily
To stir the coals, as I told long ere this,
The canon said, "Now, friend, you do amiss.
This is not heaped up as it ought to be;
But I shall soon amend it," offered he.
"Now let me meddle with it for a while,
For I have pity on you, by Saint Gile.
You are too hot! I see well how you sweat.
Here! Take a cloth and wipe away the wet."
And while the priest was wiping off his face
The canon took his coal with brazen grace
And laid it carefully upon the pile
Of others glowing in the crucible,
And blew on them to make the fire burn fast.

"Now let us drink," the canon said at last,
    "For soon will all be well, I undertake.

So sit we down, and let us merry make."
And when the fire reached the wooden coal
All of the silver shavings from the hole
Fell out at once into the crucible,
As was indeed but only reasonable.
Now when this alchemist saw all was done,
"Rise up," he said, "sir priest, and go anon,
For well I know that ingot have ye none.
Fetch me a piece of chalk or a soft stone,
And I shall make a mold of the same shape
As any ingot, as I have the hope.
And also bring with you a bowl or pan
Filled up with water, and ye shall see then
How that our secret working here doth thrive.
And yet, lest ye may doubt or disbelieve
My honesty, while you are gone away,
Within your presence I shall surely stay,
And go with you, and with you come again."

The chamber door, to tell it short and plain,
They opened, and they shut, and went their way.
And to be safe they took with them the key;
And they returned again without delay.
Why should I linger all the livelong day?
He took the chalk and shaped it in the guise
Of a small ingot, as I shall advise.

The wily canon then took from his sleeve
A little tein of silver, heav'n forgive,
Which was no more than just an ounce in weight.
Now pay attention to his curséd sleight.

He shaped his ingot just as long and wide
As was this little plate, and did the deed
So slyly that the priest hath nothing spied.

And in his sleeve again he did it hide.
Now he took up the metal from the fire
And put it in the mold with merry cheer,
And in the water vessel this he cast
When he was ready. Then he bade the priest,
"Look what is there! Put in thine hand and grope.
For thou shalt find there silver, as I hope.
What? Devil of hell! Should other metal be?
Shaving of silver, silver is, pardee!"

He put his hand in and took up a tein
Of silver fine. Then glad in every vein
The priest was when he saw that it was so.
"God's blessing, and His holy Mother's, too,
And all the saints', sir canon, be upon
You," said the priest, "and I their malison
Shall bear unless, indeed, ye teach to me
This noble craft and all this subtlety.
I shall be yours in all that e'er I may."

Then said the canon, "I shall make assay
A second time, that you may well take heed
And become expert, so that in your need,
When you're alone, you may engage again
In this great science, in this discipline.
Let's take another ounce," the canon said,
"Of quicksilver, without more words indeed,
And do with it as we have done ere this
With the first ounce, which now fine silver is."

The simple priest busied himself again
To do all that the canon, curséd man,
Commanded him, and fast he blew the fire
To bring about the fruit of his desire.
And now the wily canon, all the while

Prepared the priest still further to beguile,
And for appearance, in his hand he bore
A hollow stick. Take heed, I say! Beware!
Into its end an ounce, and nothing more,
Of silver scraps he put, just as before
Were in the coal, plugged up with wax full well,
For to keep in the shavings, every deal.
And while the priest about his business went,
The canon with his stick was diligent.
He stirred the coals until the wax began
To weaken in the fire, as any man,
Unless he be a fool, knows that it must.
Then from the stick went all the silver dust
And soon into the crucible it fell.
Now, sirs, what would ye better have than well?
When thus the priest once more beguiled hath been,
Suspecting naught but truth, to tell it plain,
He was so glad that I cannot express
In any way his mirth and happiness,
And to the canon offered once again
His worldly goods. "Yea," said the canon then,
"Though I be poor, yet shrewd thou shalt me find.
I warn thee, there is more to learn behind.
Is any copper in the house?" said he.

"Yea," said the priest, "sir, well I trow there be."

"If not, then buy us some, and speedily.
Now, sir, go forth and hie thee on thy way."

He went his way and brought the copper back.
The canon in his hands the metal took
And of this copper weighed out but an ounce.
My tongue is all too simple to pronounce,

As agent of my wit, the doubleness
Of this false canon, flow'r of cursédness.

He put the ounce of copper in the pot
And on the fire quickly hath it set,
Threw in the powder, made the priest to blow,
And in his working bend him over low
As he had done before. All was a jape.
Just as he wished, he made the priest his ape.
And after, in the mold he hath it cast,
And in the pan of water at the last
He put it, and he put in his own hand.
And in his sleeve (as you will understand;
You've heard before) he had a silver tein.
He slyly took it out, this curséd man
(The priest unwitting of his craft and guile)
And in the bottom of the pan the while
He let it lie, while he groped to and fro,
And wondrous privately took up also
The copper tein (still innocent the priest)
And hid it. Then he took him by the breast
And to him spake, and thus said in his game,
"Stoop down, good sir, or else you are to blame!
Help me now here, as I helped you before.
Put in your hand and see what may be there."

The priest took up the silver plate anon.
Then said the canon, "Sir, let us be gone
With these three teins, these plates which we have
    wrought,
Unto a smith, to learn if they be aught.
For, by my faith, I know not as I should
Whether they be of silver fine and good.
But quickly proven shall this metal be."

Unto a goldsmith with these pieces three
They went, and put the silver in assay
By fire and hammer. No man might say nay,
For they were all that they were meant to be.

This sotted priest, who happier than he?
Thus to the canon he hath spoke and said,
"For love of God, Who for us all hath died,
And as I may deserve it here of you,
What shall this secret cost me? Tell me true."

"By'r Lady," said the canon, "it is dear.
I warn you well. Except me and a friar,
In all of England no man this can make."

"No matter," cried the priest. "For heaven's sake,
What must I pay you? Tell it me, I pray."

"Indeed," he said, "it is full dear, I say.
Sir, in one word, if you this lore would have,
You shall pay forty pounds, as God me save!
But for the kindness that you did for me,
You should pay many more, in certainty."

The priest the sum of forty pounds at once
In nobles fetched and took them, every ounce,
Unto the canon for this same receipt.
But all his words were nothing but deceit.

Then quoth the canon, "Farewell! *Grand merci!*"
He went his way. The priest after that day
Saw him no more. But now, when'er he would
Make silver out of copper as he should
With this receipt, farewell! It would not be!
Lo, thus defrauded and beguiled was he.

Three Men in Search of Death

The Pardoner's Tale

Thise ryotoures three, of whiche I telle,
Longe erst er pryme rong of any belle,
Were set hem in a taverne for to drinke;
And as they satte, they herde a belle clinke
Biforn a cors, was caried to his grave . . .

The description of the Pardoner in "The Prologue" shows him up as a greedy and disreputable person. When it is his turn to tell a tale, the company asks him for something moral. Thereupon, he produces a sermon about the sin of avarice, his own great fault, and ends it with a short illustrative story. Versions of this story have been found in Oriental as well as European folklore.

As Chaucer tells it, this is considered one of the greatest short stories of all time. He sets the narrative against the background of the Black Death, which ravaged England many times during the fourteenth century. An atmosphere of doom builds up to the final tragedy. Chaucer adds depth to his mystery by failing to identify the Old Man who is unable to die. Is he Death? Is he not?

Three drunken roisterers of whom I tell,
Long before prime was rung by any bell,
Had set them in a tavern for to drink;
And as they sat, they heard a death bell clink
Before a coffin carried to the grave.
One of the brawlers shouted to his knave,
"Run out," he cried. "Inquire readily
What corpse is this that here is passing by.
And look that thou report his name aright."

"Sir," said the boy, "I need not stir a mite.
'Twas told me ere ye came, a full two hours;
He was, pardee, a former friend of yours;
And of a sudden he was slain tonight
As he lay drunk upon his chimney-seat.
There came a sneaking thief that men call Death,
That in this country all the people slay'th,
And with his spear he smote his heart in two
And went his way in silence even so.
With pestilence he hath a thousand slain.
And, master, ere you look upon him plain,
Methinketh it were truly necessary
That you beware of such an adversary:
Be ready for to meet him ever more.
For thus my dame hath taught me. Now, no more!"

"By Holy Mary," said the taverner,
"The boy speaks true, for he hath slain this year
In a great village hence about a mile
Man, woman, child and servant, great and small.
I trow his habitation must be there.
To be on guard, indeed, great wisdom 'twere,
Lest he should do dishonor to a man."

"Yea?" cried this drunken roisterer again.
"Is it such peril with this thief to meet?
I'll seek him out in byway and in street;
I swear it by the holy bones of God.
We three are one, my friends. Now hear my word.
Let each of us hold up his hand to the other,
And each of us become the other's brother,
And we will slay this faithless traitor, Death.
He shall be slain, he that so many slay'th,
By God's own dignity, ere it be night."

Together then these three have made their plight
To live and die each one of them for other,
As if he had been born his very brother,
And up they started, drunk and raging so,
To that same village on their way to go
Of which the tavern-keeper spoke before.
And many a foul and grisly oath they swore.

When they had gone not fully half a mile,
Just as they would have stepped across a stile,
They came upon an old man, poorly dressed,
Who with an humble greeting them addressed
And said to them, "God look upon you, sirs!"

Thereon the proudest of these roisterers
Answered again, "What? Churl with sorry grace,
Why art thou thus all covered save thy face?
Why hast thou lived so long, so many a year?"

The ancient man looked in his visage there
And said thus, "For, alas, I cannot find
A man, although I walk as far as Ind,
Either in village or in city street,

Willing to change his youth for my estate;
And therefore all my years I carry still
As long a time as it shall be God's will.

"Not even Death will have my life, alas!
Thus I walk like a captive without peace,
And on the ground, which is my mother's gate,
With this my staff I knock, early and late,
And cry, 'Belovéd mother, let me in!
Lo, how I wither, flesh and blood and skin!
Alas, when shall my body come to rest?
Mother, with you I would exchange the chest
That in my chamber now too long doth lie,
Yea, for a haircloth shroud to cover me!'
But yet for me she will not do this grace.
And so full pale and shrunken is my face.

"But, sirs, for you it is no courtesy
To speak to an old man such villainy,
Unless he harm you in some word or deed.
In Holy Writ yourselves you well may read,
'For an old man with hoarfrost on his head,
You should arise.' Now, be admonishéd.
Harm to an agéd man thou should'st not do
More than you would that men should do to you
If you desire to old age to bide.
Now, God be with you, where you walk or ride.
I must go thither where I have to go."

"Nay, ancient churl, by God thou shalt not so,"
Then said another boaster there anon.
"Thou partest not so lightly, by Saint John!
Thou spake just now of that same traitor Death
That in this country all the people slay'th.

Have here my oath, as thou must be his spy!
Tell where he is, or dearly shalt thou buy
Thy freedom, by the holy sacrament!
For thou art one of his and doth assent
To slay us younger folk, thou faithless thief!"

"Now, sirs," quoth he, "if that ye be so lief
To meet with Death, turn up this crookéd way,
For in that grove I left him, by my fay,
Under a tree, and there he will abide.
Not for your boasting will he run and hide.
See ye that oak? Right there ye may him find.
And may God save you, Who hath saved mankind,
And better you!" Thus said this agéd man.

Now every one of these three brawlers ran
Until he reached the tree, and there they found
Of florins coined of fine gold, minted round,
Well nigh to eight full bushels, as they thought.
No longer then indeed for Death they sought.
But each of them was gladdened at the sight,
Because the florins were so fair and bright,
And down they set them by the precious hoard.
The worst of all the three said the first word.

"Brethren," quoth he, "take heed of what I say.
My wit is great, although I jest and play.
Fortune this treasure unto us doth give,
In mirth and jollity our lives to live.
And lightly as it comes, so shall it speed.
And, by God's worth, who would have thought,
     indeed,
Today that we should have so fair a grace?
But should this gold be carried from this place

Home to my house, or otherwise to yours—
Because we know so well this gold is ours—
Then were we all in high felicity.
But certainly by day this may not be,
For folk would say that we were in the wrong
And for our treasure suffer us to hang.
This gold must then be carried home by night,
As secretly and slyly as it might.
Therefore I counsel that among us all
We draw for lots, and where the cut shall fall,
He that hath drawn the lot, with merry heart
Shall run into the town, and that full smart,
And bring us bread and wine full privily,
While two of us shall keep a watchful eye
Upon the gold; and if he does not tarry,
When it is night, this treasure we will carry
By full agreement where we think it best."

This one now held the lots within his fist
And bade them draw and see where it should fall;
And it fell on the youngest of them all.
And forth toward the town he hastened then.
And thereupon, as soon as he was gone,
The one of them spoke thus unto the other,
"Thou know'st well thou'rt sworn to be my brother.
Thy profit here I'll tell to thee anon.
Thou know'st indeed our friend to town is gone;
And here is gold, and that abundantly,
That now should be divided among three.
But nonetheless if I can shape it so
That it should be divided among two,
Have I not done a friendly turn for thee?"

The other one replied, "How may this be?
He knows the gold was left between us two.
What can we say to him? What can we do?"

"Can you keep counsel?" said the former shrew.
"And I shall tell thee, in a word or two,
What we can do to bring this all about."

"I grant," replied the other, "out of doubt,
That, by my troth, I will no traitor be."

"Now," quoth the first, "thou know'st that two
    are we,
And two of us are stronger far than one.
Look well. When he returns, then right anon
Arise as if to wrestle him in jest,
And I shall stick my dagger through his breast
While you are struggling with him as in game.
And with your knife, then look you do the same.
And then shall all this gold divided be,
My dearest fellow, between me and thee.
Then may we both our pleasures all fulfill,
And play at dice as often as we will."
And thus these roisterers agree to slay
Their fellow thief, as ye have heard me say.

The youngest, he that went into the town,
Full often in his heart rolled up and down
The beauty of the florins new and bright.
"O Lord," he thought, "if only that I might
Have all this treasure to myself alone,
There'd be no man that lives beneath the throne
Of God that lived so merrily as I."
And at the last the Fiend, our enemy,

Put in his mind that he should poison buy
With which his two companions he might slay.
So forth he went, no longer would he tarry,
Into the town to an apothecary
And begged him earnestly that he should sell
Him now some poison drug, that he might kill
The rats and, furthermore, a polecat who
Had slain his capons and his hens also;
For he would fain avenge him, if he might,
On vermin that destroyed his flocks by night.

Th'apothecary answered, "Thou shalt have
A potion that, as God my soul shall save,
In all this world there is no living creature
Who drinks or swallows any of this mixture,
A drop no bigger than a grain of corn,
But he shall forfeit all his life anon.
Yea, die he shall, and in a lesser while
Than thou couldst walk a pace and not a mile.
This poison is so strong and violent."

This curséd man, as was his vile intent,
Took up the poison potion, and he ran
Into a nearby street, unto a man
And borrowed from the latter bottles three;
In two of these the drug decanted he.
He kept the third one clean, to drink himself,
For all the night he planned to dig and delve
In carrying the treasure from its place.
And when this roisterer, with sorry grace,
Had filled with wine his heavy bottles three,
To his companions once more hastened he.

What need is there to sermon of it more?
For just as they had planned his death before,

Just so in little time they have him slain.
And when this was accomplished, spoke the one,
"Now let us sit and drink and make us merry,
And afterward we shall his body bury."

And with that word, it happed to be the case,
He took the bottle where the poison was
And drank, and gave his friend to drink also,
For which anon they perished, both these two.

But Avicenna never, I suppose,
Wrote in a canon or a book of prose
No worse description of empoisoning
Than had these wretches ere their perishing.
Thus ended then these homicides, these two,
And thus with them their poisoner also!

Glossary and Notes

abbot: the head of a community of monks of a religious order

abide: stay, remain

accord: agreement

accordant: suitable, auspicious

Aeneid: epic poem by Vergil, Roman poet of the first century B.C. describing the travels of Aeneas, a Trojan prince who established the Latin race after the fall of Troy

afeard: afraid, frightened

affray: disaster, cause for fear

affright, affrighted: afraid, frightened

aghast: horrified, appalled

aketon: a short tunic worn under a coat of mail, sometimes a coat of mail

alchemy: the "science" of transmuting base metals into gold. See the preface to the Clerk in "The Prologue."

alderman: a member of a city council

alehouse stake: a stake or post outside a wine shop or alehouse. Garlands were often hung upon these as tavern signs.

Alexandria: In the description of the Knight in "The Prologue," we find the names of many places in which campaigns and battles were fought during Chaucer's lifetime and in which a knight might well have taken part. I have purposely cut out a number of these. The English Earl of Derby laid siege to Granada in Spain in 1343 and captured Algeciras in 1344 from the Moors. Pierre de Lusignan, sometimes called King Peter of Cyprus, undertook many campaigns against the enemies of Christianity during the 1360's. In 1365 he took Alexandria in Egypt. This King Peter visited the English court during the early 1360's, when Chaucer was attached to the royal household. Tramissene (Tlemcen) in western Algeria was the scene of fighting between Christians and Moslems during the fourteenth century. Our Knight, after his service with Pierre de Lusignan, may have borne arms with the Teutonic Knights, a feudal society with headquarters in northern Germany, which extended its hold over northeastern Europe, especially over Lithuania and Russia, during the latter part of the century. His being served before all others at the feast in Prussia indicates that he was held in high esteem and honored at the special feast of the Teutonic Knights, the Table of Honor.

Algeciras: See note on Alexandria.

alight: alighted, dismounted

ambler: a horse that ambles, probably an old workhorse

amiss: wrongly

Amor vincit omnia (Latin): Love conquers all

Amphion, King: a king of Thebes in ancient Greece. He played the lyre so beautifully that the very stones lifted themselves into the wall he built around the city.

annunciate: foretold, prophesied

anon: at once, shortly, soon

apace: quickly, in a hurry

Apollo: the God of light in classical mythology, sometimes called Phoebus; the sun

apothecary: druggist, pharmacist

archer's guard: an armlet of leather to protect the inner arm from being scraped by the bowstring

aright: all right

Aristotle: Greek philosopher of the fourth century B.C.

armor-coat: a tunic worn over armor, generally embroidered with a knight's escutcheon or coat-of-arms

Armoric: Armorica, a name for Brittany, province or duchy in the northwest corner of France

array: clothing or gear; splendor

Artois: See note on Flanders.

ascendant: the point of the Zodiac rising above the horizon and therefore affecting human nature at a particular time, according to astrology

assay: test, submit to analysis

assent: agree, consent; agreement

assize: a session of a court held periodically in the shires in England, presided over by a justice who represented the King rather than the local lord

astrology: the "science" of foretelling human fortunes by the stars

aught: anything

Avicenna: Arabian philosopher and author of a treatise on medicine in the eleventh century A.D.

awry: amiss, wrongly

aye: always

azure: blue

Babylon: ancient city on the Euphrates River, capital of the Chaldean Empire

bachelor: candidate for knighthood, candidate for an academic degree

baldric: a strap worn over the shoulder

bare of thread: threadbare, worn

battlemented: notched like the wall of a parapet with spaces from which the defenders might shoot at an approaching enemy

befall: happen

beguile: deceive

Bell: an inn near the Tabard in Southwark

Benedicité (Latin): God bless us!

Benedict: St. Benedict. See the preface to the Monk in "The Prologue."

benefice: church assignment, the living of a priest

benignity: kindness, virtue

bereave: take away from

beseech (*besought*): beg (begged)

bestride: straddle

bethought: ("am bethought") have thought of

betide: happen

bier: resting place for a corpse

blancmanger: literally, white food; a dish made of chicken and cream

blissful: blessed

Bologna: a city in northern Italy

bonnily: prettily, pleasantly

Boulogne: a city on the northern coast of France

bower: chamber or sleeping quarters, usually in a castle

box: ("made of brass and box") boxwood

brand: torch

bream: a fish

Brittany: former duchy in the northwest corner of France, washed by the Bay of Biscay and the English Channel

Bruges cloth: cloth woven in the city of Bruges in Flanders

buckler: shield

bull, papal: a letter of instruction from the Pope

burgess: a citizen of a town or city

canon: a clergyman attached to a cathedral, a member of a religious order

Canterbury: a town in Kent in southern England. The Cathedral here was established by St. Augustine in 597 A.D. See the preface to "The Prologue."

carbuncle: a precious stone of a red color

carl: rascal, fellow

Cato: Dionysius Cato, Latin author of the third or fourth century A.D., whose works were studied by medieval schoolboys

cell: cloister, monastery; domain

centaury: herb with medicinal properties

cetewale: a plant of the ginger family, used for seasoning

Chaldea: ancient empire in the valley of the Tigris and Euphrates Rivers. Its capital was Babylon.

chamberlain: steward in a royal or noble household

chantry: endowment to pay a priest to sing masses for a departed soul

chapelaine: nun who acted as a personal attendant upon a prioress

charger: war horse

chattels: possessions, personal property

Cheap: Cheapside, the market district of London

cheer: ("with humble cheer") face, facial expression

cherubic: like a cherub. The folk of the Middle Ages

pictured the cherubim, or second rank of angels, as having bright red faces.

chivachy: cavalry expedition

chivalry: the code by which knights lived. See the preface to the Knight in "The Prologue."

choler: yellow bile, one of the four humors that affected health and temperament, according to medieval medicine. See the preface to "Chanticleer and the Fox."

Christendom: the Christian world

Christopher: a medal of St. Christopher, the patron saint of foresters and travelers

churl: peasant, boor

ciclatoun: expensive material for clothing

clarion: a kind of trumpet with a high, clear tone

clerk: a member of the clergy; a student preparing for holy orders

coat-of-arms: heraldic emblems or bearings identifying a noble family, an escutcheon

coat-of-mail: tunic of metal fabric to protect the body in battle

coffer: chest to hold clothing, gold, or other possessions

Cologne: a city in Germany

compeer: companion

complaint: ("songs and complaints") poem, lyric, telling of a sad state of affairs

confrere: companion, colleague

consecrate: consecrated, devoted

constable: a high officer of the king; the keeper of a castle

cordwain: Cordovan leather

cot: cottage

counterfeit: imitate

courser: a fast horse

coverchiefs: kerchiefs, cloths worn over the head. The Wife's coverchiefs, according to some authorities, were considered old-fashioned in the late 1300's and not nearly so stylish as the pleated wimple worn by Madame Eglentine.

coy: quiet, shy. The word did not mean flirtatious in Chaucer's English.

Creed: the Apostle's Creed

crest: helmet

Croesus: King of Lydia in Asia Minor, conquered by Cyrus, King of the Persians, in 546 B.C. He was famous for his wealth.

crops: ("the tender crops") young plants or shoots

crucible: a pot of porcelain or clay used for melting ore and metal

cubit: a measure of length, originally the distance from a man's elbow to the tip of his middle finger, eighteen inches

cumin seed: an aromatic seed used as a flavoring

Cyrus: the founder of the Persian Empire, conqueror of Lydia and later of Chaldea

dainty: costly, valuable; delicate; nice

dais: a raised platform

dale: valley

dame: ("My dame hath taught me") mother

Dame: ("Dame Dorigen") Lady

Daniel: Hebrew prophet. See the Book of Daniel in the *Old Testament.*

deal: bit; ("every deal") every little bit

dear: costly, expensive; expensively

debonaire: pleasing, charming

decant: pour, especially into a bottle

deem: suppose, know

degree: ("each in his degree") social rank

degree: ("When fifteen degrees had been ascended") degrees of a circle, especially of the equinoctial circle traveled by the sun around the earth, according to astrologists. Fifteen degrees constitute one twenty-fourth of three hundred and sixty degrees; therefore, they mark the passing of one hour.

Delphi: the site of the oracle and temple of Apollo in Greece

demeanor: manner

devise: contrive, arrange, make; describe, narrate

distaff: a staff on which the raw flax is held in spinning yarn

dole: sorrow, pain

doth: does

doublet: shirt, jacket

doughty: strong, valiant, capable

down: ("by dale and eke by down") hill

draught: drink, swallow

dung: manure

eke: also

elate: proud

else: ("if else") otherwise

enow: enough

Epicurus: a Greek philosopher of the third century B.C., who held that the aim of philosophy was to make men happy. By happiness he meant peace of mind and freedom from anguish. His teachings were misinterpreted to mean that the pleasures of good living—eating and drinking—were the highest good.

ere: before

espy: see

estate: social rank; circumstances
Evangelist, Book of the: the Gospels
Faéry: Fairyland
fain: glad, willing, happy; gladly, willingly
farthing: a small coin; a tiny speck or bit
fathom: a measure of length or depth; six feet
fay: faith; ("by my fay") by my faith
fee simple: title to land clear of liens and mortgages
feign: pretend
feint: a mock blow intended to distract the opponent's attention
felony: crime
fiend: devil
Fiend: Satan, the Devil
figure: figure of speech
Flanders: a province or duchy in what are now the Low Countries, Holland and Belgium ("In Flanders, in Artois, or Picardy"). After the Treaty of 1360 between the English and the French, fighting ceased for a time, but it broke out again in 1369 and from time to time thereafter. The Squire may well have taken part in some of these skirmishes of the Hundred Years' War, as did Chaucer in his youth. See the Introduction.
Fleming: a citizen of Flanders, a member of the Flemish colony in London. Many Flemings were killed during the Peasants' Revolt in 1381 led by Jack Straw because of the popular belief that they took work from English weavers.
flesh: meat
florins: gold coins, originally issued in Florence in Italy but later minted in England during the reign of Edward III

fluting: playing the flute

forsooth: in truth, indeed

franklin: a free man. See the preface to the Franklin in "The Prologue."

fumitory: an herb sometimes used as a tonic

furlong: a measure of distance, now two hundred and twenty yards

Galicia: northwestern Spain, home of the famous shrine of St. James, Santiago de Compostela

galingale: a flavoring

Ganelon: vassal of Charlemagne who betrayed his trust and caused the death of Roland at the hands of the Saracens, according to *The Song of Roland*

gauds: the large beads in a rosary, used in saying the Pater Nosters

gillyflower: the clove pink, a fragrant spice

girdle: belt

Gironde: a river of France emptying into the Bay of Biscay

girt: girdled, tied around

glee: song, merriment

goshawk: a large, short-winged hawk used in falconry

Gospel: the Bible

grace: favor, mercy, kindness

Granada: a city in Spain. See the note on Alexandria.

Grand merci! (French): Many thanks!

ground: ("of ground") term used to describe the thread count in fabric

guerdon: reward

guild: association of members of a craft or trade; religious or social organization

Guildhall: meeting hall of the Corporation of the City of London *guildsmen:* members of a guild

guise: manner, way

haberdasher: a merchant who deals in clothing

habergeon: coat-of-mail

haircloth: rough, stiff cloth of camel's or horse's hair, often used in shrouds

hart: male deer

hast: have

hath: has

hauberk: coat-of-mail. In the description of Sir Thopas, the word may mean a breastplate worn over a coat-of-mail, or it may mean that our hero wore two sets of chain mail.

heath: meadow

Heathenness: the lands ruled by the Moslems—Arabs, Moors, and Turks

heed: attention

hellebore: a medicinal herb

helm: helmet

hent: grasped, taken

hie: hasten, hurry

hight: named, called

hip: ("beareth the red hip") berry

holt: wood, woodland

Holy Paul's: St. Paul's Cathedral in London

Holy Writ: the Bible

Hosanna!: Praise to the Lord!

hose: tights

hostel, hostelry: inn, hotel

hue: color

humors: the four fluids that determined a person's health, according to medieval medicine. See the preface to "Chanticleer and the Fox."

Ind: India

indite: compose, write

ingot: a mold in which metal is cast

In principio mulier est hominis confusio (Latin): First
. of all, woman is the confusion of man

Inn of Temple: Inn of Court. See the preface to the
Manciple in "The Prologue."

intoning: chanting, singing

ire: anger

Iscariot: Judas Iscariot who betrayed Jesus Christ

Israel: the northern kingdom of the Hebrews of the *Old
Testament*

iwiss: certainly, indeed

jane: a small coin

Janus: the God of Entrances for whom January is
named, portrayed as having two faces, one on the
back of his head, in classical mythology

jape: trick, deceit

jay: a bird

Jerusalem: the chief city of the Holy Land

Jewish work: fine workmanship. Jews were among the
best armorers in Europe.

Jonah: Hebrew prophet who was swallowed by a whale
and cast up after three days. His story is told in the
Book of Jonah in the *Old Testament.*

joust: fight on horseback in a mock battle or tournament

Judges: a book of the *Old Testament*

Jupiter: Roman name of the King of the Gods in classical mythology

keeper of the cell: administrative officer of a monastery

Kerru: a village in Brittany

kirtle: shirt, underwear

knave: boy, page, servant; a boy-child

Knight-of-Shire: Member of Parliament

Koran: the sacred book of Islam, the Mohammedan religion

lack: fault, cause for complaint; insufficiency

lancegay: a slender lance or spear

latten: a brasslike metal, alloy; tin

laurel: a shrub

lay: song, ballad

lief: willing, willingly

liege: the overlord to whom a knight gave service

lineage: family, ancestry; noble birth

list: desire, desired

lists: jousting-place, the arena in which a tournament is held

Lithuania: a land in eastern Europe. See the note on Alexandria.

livery: uniform; retinue, a lord's following

logic: a branch of philosophy, the study of inductive reasoning, originated by Aristotle, the Greek philosopher

Lombardy: province, once a kingdom, in northern Italy

lore: learning, education, knowledge

love-knot: a knot or bow of ribbon or fine metal, usually given as a token of affection by one lover to another

Lucine, Lucina: name given to Diana, Goddess of the Moon, twin sister of Apollo, in classical mythology

lusty: ardent, vigorous, zealous; happy, joyous

Lydia: ancient kingdom in Asia Minor

mace: club, often with spikes in the head, used as a weapon

Mahomet: Mahommed, prophet of Islam

mail: ("coat-of-mail") fabric knitted or woven from metal chains

malison: curse, denunciation

manciple: steward of a club, college, or Inn of Court. See the preface to the Manciple in "The Prologue."

mansions of the moon: the twenty-eight sections into which the moon's monthly course is divided, according to astrology. A special knowledge of these mansions enabled the possessor to work feats of magic.

mantle: cloak

marchioness: the wife of a marquis

mark: a gold or silver coin worth thirteen shillings and fourpence

marquis: an hereditary nobleman ranking above a count and below a duke

marshal: an officer of the royal household, a majordomo or chief steward

Maur: a disciple of St. Benedict. See the preface to the Monk in "The Prologue."

mead: meadow; a fermented drink made with honey

meed: a reward or gift

melancholy: black bile, one of the four humors that affected human health, according to medieval medicine. See the preface to "Chanticleer and the Fox."

merciable: merciful

mercury: a metallic element, quicksilver

methinketh: I think

mew: coop, cage; barnyard

mien: manner, behavior, expression

minstrelsy: the art and practice of minstrels; singing and playing; musical instruments *morrow:* morning, the next day

mortify: (in alchemy) to transmute, to change one substance to another

motley: cloth woven in parti-colored design

nativity: birth

naught: nothing, not at all

Nebuchadnezzar: King of Babylon, or Chaldea, during the sixth century B.C. He conquered Jerusalem and carried many Hebrew nobles, including the prophet Daniel, to Babylon. He went mad during the last part of his life. His story is told in the Book of Daniel in the *Old Testament.*

Nineveh: ancient city on the Tigris River, which figures in the story of Jonah, the Hebrew prophet, in the Book of Jonah in the *Old Testament*

Noel!: a shout of joy at Christmas

nonce: the occasion, the time being. "For the nonce" may mean "for the time being," or it may be used to give emphasis to a statement.

nonetheless: nevertheless

Northumberland: county in northeastern England on the North Sea

oratory: chapel for private prayers

orison: prayer

Orleans: city and university center on the Loire River in France

outrider: the member of a monastic community who took care of the outside business, overseeing the use of the land, selling produce, buying supplies, etc.

Oxenford: Oxford

pace: move forward; surpass

pagan: unbeliever

palfrey: saddle horse

palmers: religious persons who have made pilgrimages to Jerusalem. They carried palm leaves brought from the Holy Land.

pandemain: fine white bread

Panicia: an unindentified area, apparently in the neighborhood of Bologna in northern Italy

paramour: lover

pardee: a common oath of exclamation, "for heaven's sake!"

pardoner: a friar authorized to sell pardons. See the preface to the Pardoner in "The Prologue."

pardons: documents allegedly obtained from the Pope granting forgiveness for sins. See the preface to the Pardoner in "The Prologue."

Parvise: the porch of St. Paul's Cathedral in London, where lawyers gathered to consult clients, discuss cases, and settle certain types of civil actions

penance: punishment for a sin confessed to a priest

pestilence: the Black Death, a plague that ravaged England several times during Chaucer's lifetime; a curse

Peter's boat: the boat in which Peter and the other disciples were sailing when Christ appeared to them walking on the water. See Matthew XIV, 29, in the *New Testament.*

philosopher: a student of the nature of the universe. In the Middle Ages the word was used also in a slang sense to mean alchemist.

philosophy: the study of the principles that regulate the universe; learning, knowledge; in slang, the practice of alchemy

Phoebus: Apollo, the God of Light in classical mythology; the sun *physic:* medicine

Picardy: a province in northern France. See the note on Flanders.

pike: a fish

pilgrim: traveler to a shrine. See the preface to "The Prologue."

pilgrimage: journey to a shrine. See the preface to "The Prologue."

piteous: full of pity; pitiable

pittance: payment, originally the food given to a begging friar

plate: sheets of metal used in armor

plight: pledge

poleaxe: long-handled battle-ax

polecat: a small animal like a ferret who preys on poultry, not a skunk

Poperinghe: a town in Flanders, center of the weaving industry. See the preface to "The Ballad of Sir Thopas."

popinjay: a parrot

pottage: stew of meat and vegetables, rich soup

powder-marchant: a spice with a tart flavor

Priam, King: the King of Troy during the Trojan War, according to the *Iliad* and the *Aeneid*

pricketh: stirs, arouses

prime: the hour beginning at 6 A.M.; the earliest part of the day; the best years of one's life

privily: privately, secretly

Prussia: land in north central Europe on the Baltic Sea. See the note on Alexandria.

psaltery: musical instrument like a harp

Pyrrhus: son of Achilles. He killed King Priam in the

final destruction of Troy by the Greeks, according to the *Aeneid*.

Python: a serpent who laid waste the region of Delphi in ancient Greece. He was slain by Apollo, who claimed the spot as the site of his oracle, according to classical mythology.

Questio quid juris? (Latin): I question what law (you're talking about)—a phrase used by lawyers

quick: ("not fully quick") alive

quicksilver: mercury, a metal

quirboilly: leather boiled to make it hard

quoth: said

raconteur: storyteller

ram: male sheep, often given as a prize in a wrestling match

Ram: ("within the Ram") Aries, the first sign of the Zodiac. According to astrologers, the sun began its journey through a series of twelve signs, or constellations, in March.

ready: ("ready me") prepare, make ready

receipt: recipe, formula

relics: clothing or bones of saints, often thought to perform miracles

renown: fame

rent: income; torn, split

rewel-bone: whalebone

roisterer: reveler, wastrel

rote: a musical instrument; memory; ("by rote,") by heart

Rouncival: the hospital of St. Mary of Rouncivalle in London

roundel: a song or poem with a repeated refrain

roundelay: a song or poem like a roundel
rout: following; crowd of people
rue: regret
rueful: sorry, sad
Russia: country in eastern Europe. See the note on Alexandria.
ruth: pity
sable: black
saffron: yellow
St. Anna: St. Anne, the mother of the Virgin Mary
St. Gile: unidentified saint; an oath
St. James in Galicia: Santiago de Compostela in Spain, a famous shrine possessing the relics of St. James
St. Julian: the patron saint of hospitality
St. Loy: St. Eligius, an obscure saint, patron of goldsmiths; a very mild oath
St. Marie: the Virgin Mary
St. Paul: one of the apostles and author of several books of the *New Testament*
St. Thomas' Watering: a point on the Kent Road out of London at which travelers paused to rest and water their horses
Saluzzo: a town in northeastern Italy, once the capital of a land ruled by a marquis
Samson: hero of the early Israelites. His story, which Chaucer follows closely, is told in the Book of Judges in the *Old Testament*.
sanguine: red
scabbard: a sheath for a sword
see: ("sovereign see") throne, capital city
seemly: handsome, pleasant, fitting
seethe: boil, poach

179

seigniory: the territory over which a lord holds dominion

Seine: a river in France emptying into the English Channel

sergeant: a personal attendant; a military officer of the lower rank

Sergeant-at-Law: one of a very small group of barristers in medieval England chosen by the King as his legal representatives. See the preface to the Sergeant of the Law in "The Prologue."

sessions: meetings of the Justices of the Peace

sheriff: the King's administrative officer in an English shire

shire: an English county

shrew: rascal

shriven: forgiven for one's sins

shroud: a garment for the dead

Sinon: the Greek who persuaded the Trojans to bring the wooden horse into their city and thus betrayed them into inviting their own destruction, according to the *Iliad*

Sir Olifant: Sir Elephant

Sir Percival: an unidentified knight whose adventures were presumably known to Chaucer's audience

sire: father; older man; term of respect

slake: satisfy, diminish

smart: feel pain, suffer; quickly

smite: strike

sooth: truth; ("in sooth") in truth

sop in wine: piece of bread soaked in wine

sotted: infatuated, foolish

Southwark: once a suburb of London at the south end of London Bridge, now a part of the city. See the preface to "The Prologue."

sovereign: royal; king

span: measure of length, formerly the width of a person's hand

spicery: spices

spill: spend; shed

steven: voice

stew: fishpond, tank

stewards: caretakers, managers

stile: a set of steps for climbing over a fence or wall

stint: delay, stop

strand: seashore

Stratford atte Bow: a village once east of London, now swallowed up by the city. Here there was a Benedictine nunnery, St. Leonard's, at which the Prioress may have been educated. The French spoken there was obviously not pure Parisian French but the Norman French of a London suburb.

Straw, Jack: a leader of the Peasants' Revolt in 1381. See the note on *Fleming.*

succor: help

summoner: an officer of the church court. See the preface to the Summoner in "The Prologue."

sundry: various, of many kinds

surcoat: overcoat

surety: dowry

Susannah: a maiden falsely accused of evil behavior by two elders. Her story is told in the Apocrypha books of the Bible.

symphony: musical instruments in general; a little drum

Syria: a country in Asia at the eastern end of the Mediterranean Sea

Tabard: an inn in Southwark. See the preface to "The Prologue."

tackle: gear, tools, instruments used in a trade or craft

tapicer: tapestry maker

targe: an archery target; a large shield

Taurus: the Bull, the second sign of the Zodiac, entered by the sun about April 20, according to astrology

tein: tain, a small metal plate or rod; a piece of tin

Termagaunt: a supposed heathen god

thee: you

thither: to that place

thorp: a small village or hamlet

thou: you

thrall: slavery

thriftily: efficiently, expertly

thrifty: serviceable, useful

thrustle, thrustlecock: thrush

timbre: the character or resonance of a voice

tithes: the tenth part of a person's income, which was owed to the church. It was an all-too-frequent practice for priests to threaten their parishioners with excommunication or eternal damnation if the latter failed to pay their tithes.

Toledo, tables of: astrological tables prepared at Toledo in Spain, used in working magic

Tramissene: a city (Tlemcen) in western Algeria. See note on Alexandria.

troth: truth; faith, faithfulness; promise, pledge; ("by my troth") by my faith

trow: believe

undertake: ("I undertake") promise, guarantee

unwitting: unsuspecting, innocent

vassal: one who held land from an overlord under the feudal system, usually a knight or member of the higher nobility

Venus: Roman name of Aphrodite, the Greek Goddess of Love and Beauty; one of the planets of the solar system

vernicle: the handkerchief that St. Veronica lent to Christ to wipe His brow as He carried the Cross to Calvary. According to legend, Christ's face was imprinted upon the cloth when she retrieved it.

vestments: clothing

vigils: evening services before guild festivals or saints' days

villainy: evil, dishonor, blasphemy

virilay: a lyric poem

visage: face

Viso, Mount: highest peak in the Alps on the border between France and Italy

wallet: a purse

wastel bread: fine white bread made with wheat flour

weeds: clothes

wend: go

wide: roomy, comfortable

wight: person, human being of any social rank

William, King: Duke William of Normandy, who conquered England in 1066 and became King William I

wimple: a cloth covering worn over the head and around the neck by women of the Middle Ages, worn by nuns today

wimpled: wearing a wimple

wist: knew, known

wit: ("a ready wit") power of expressing oneself cleverly and amusingly; intelligence, good sense

withal: as well, besides; with

withsay: object to

wont: used, accustomed

worthy: noble, courageous. The line, "And although he was worthy, he was wise," has been interpreted in various ways. It may imply a sly dig at the merchant knight of Chaucer's day who was noble because of his acquired title but not very wise. On the other hand, it may mean that, although the knight was courageous, he was also prudent.

worts: plants, grasses

wot: know

Wot!: a phrase spoken by a talking bird

wrought: worked, took action

ye: you

yeoman: a free man. See the preface to the Yeoman in "The Prologue."

Ypres and Gaunt: Ypres and Ghent, cloth-making centers in Flanders.

Zephyr: the West Wind